So it goes

The Literary Journal of the Kurt Vonnegut Memorial Library

Issue No. 3

Indianapolis
2014

So It Goes
The Literary Journal of the Kurt Vonnegut Memorial Library

Editor-In-Chief
J.T. Whitehead

Editors
Jessie Howenstine
Miles Murray
William Saint
Hugh Vandivier
Julia Whitehead

Layout and Design
Sara Lunsford, Visual Gravvity

Editorial Assistant
Chris Lafave

Proofreader
Sandra Profant

About Kurt Vonnegut
William Rodney Allen

© 2014 Kurt Vonnegut Memorial Library.
All rights revert to original owners.
Permission is required for reprint.

The Emelie Building
340 N. Senate Ave.
Indianapolis, IN 46204
317.652.1954
vonnegutlibrary.org

ISSN 2324-9595
ISBN 978-0-9885117-2-9

Notes ✳ Kintsugi is the Japanese art of repairing ceramics with lacquered resin mixed with metallic powders. Originating in the 15th century, the practice celebrates an object's history and imperfections, while also keeping it in service. ✳ J. Louis Gachotte's work was submitted on his behalf by Gretchen Parker. ✳ JL Kato's work "Distilled Music" was inspired by artwork on display at the Indianapolis Museum of Art: *Girl at the Piano: Recording Sound*, by Theodore Roszak, 1935.

Acknowledgments ✳ Nelson Algren's "Hand in Hand Through the Greenery ..." was published by Seven Stories as part of the collection *The Last Carousel*, and is reprinted by permission of Dan Simon of Seven Stories Press. Donald W. Baker's poem "The Coffin" was published as part of the collection *Fought By Boys*, Xlibris Corporation (2001); it appears here with the permission of Alison Baker, executrix of Mr. Baker's literary estate. Fielding Dawson's story "The Pride of the Yankees" was published by Black Sparrow Press as part of the collection *Krazy Kat & 76 More*, and appears here with the permission of David R. Godine of Black Sparrow Books. Bruce Dethlefsen's poem "A Cell Phone Rings during Matthew Dickman's Reading" was published by Cowfeather Press as part of the collection *Unexpected Shiny Things*, and appears here with the poet's and publisher's permission. "Dave Eggers's Writing Life" was first published in *The Washington Post* and appears with the author's permission. Anselm Hollo's poem "In the Land of Art" is taken from *Notes on the Possibilities and Attractions of Existence: Selected Poems 1965-2000*. Copyright © 2001 by Anselm Hollo. Reprinted with the permission of The Permissions Company, Inc. on behalf of Coffee House Press, www.coffeehousepress.com. Gerald Locklin's poem "Found Poem" was published in *Go West Young Toad* and appears with the poet's permission. Gerald Locklin's poem "Ernst Ludwig Kirshner: Five Tarts, 1914" was published in *Deep Meanings* and appears with the poet's permission. *Letter, Summer 1923* by Federico Garcia Lorca, copyright © Herederos de Federico Garcia Lorca, from Obras Completas (Galaxia/Gutenberg, 1996 edition). English-language translation by David Gershator, copyright © David Gershator and Herederos de Federico Garcia Lorca. All rights reserved. For information regarding rights and permissions of all of Lorca's works, please contact lorca@artslaw.co.uk or William Peter Kosmas, Esq., 8 Franklin Square, London W14 9UU, England; Tel: +44 020 7386 9666; Email: kosmas@artslaw.co.uk. Bonnie Maurer's poem "The Poem Stands on its Head by the Window" has been accepted for print in *War, Literature & the Arts*, as well as *Indy Writes Books;* it appears with the poet's permission. t. kilgore splake's poem "hip gallerinas" was published by Presa Press as part of the collection splake fishing in america, and appears with the permission of Eric Greinke, editor and publisher of Presa Press. James Alexander Thom's "Rejection Flip" was first published in the *Author's Guild Bulletin*, Spring, 2004, and appears with the author's permission. Richard Vargas's poem "salvation" was first published in the collection *Guernica Revisited*, published by Press 53, 2014, and appears with the poet's permission. Emile Verhaeren's poems from "The Hours of the Afternoon" first appeared in *The Love Poems of Emile Verhaeren*, a Nabu Public Domain Reprint. Nanette Vonnegut's piece originally appeared in *Kurt Vonnegut Drawings* (Monacelli Press) and appears with the author's and publisher's permission. Don Wentworth's poem from *Past All Traps* appears with the poet's permission. All Vonnegut quotes appear by permission of Don Farber, attorney for the literary estate of Kurt Vonnegut.

JOHN CLARK

__Bergeron. Harrison Bergeron.__

About Kurt Vonnegut

Kurt Vonnegut, Jr. was born November 11, 1922 in Indianapolis, the youngest of three children. The fortunes of the family changed during the Depression when Kurt Sr. saw his architectural business disappear. He sold the family home and took Kurt Jr. out of private school, where, in kindergarten, Kurt met Jane Cox, who eventually became his wife. This change in economic circumstances caused Kurt Sr. virtually to give up on life and his wife Edith to become addicted to alcohol and prescription drugs.

At Shortridge High, Vonnegut wrote for the student paper, *The Echo,* and continued his interest in journalism at Cornell, becoming managing editor of the student paper, *The Sun.* When World War II broke out, Vonnegut was 16. At 20, he entered the army and was sent to Europe, where he was captured by the Germans in the Battle of the Bulge. He was sent as a POW to Dresden, where on February 13, 1945, British and American bombers destroyed the city by dropping explosives followed by incendiary bombs. The resulting firestorm turned the non-militarized city into an inferno that killed up to 60,000 civilians. Vonnegut and his fellow POWs survived by accident only because they were housed some sixty feet underground in a slaughterhouse. Vonnegut's job after the bombing was to gather up and burn the remains of the dead. His experience at Dresden marked him for life and resulted in his literary masterpiece, *Slaughterhouse-Five.* Another sorrow of the war years was the suicide by drug overdose in 1944 of Vonnegut's mother.

After the war Vonnegut married Jane Cox, and they had three children: Mark, Edith, and Nanette. Vonnegut took a job at General Electric but began writing short fiction on the side. In 1952 his dystopian apprentice novel *Player Piano* was published. Vonnegut's beloved sister Alice Adams died of cancer in 1957, just two days after her husband had been killed in a freak commuter train crash. Kurt and Jane took in three of Alice's children, doubling the size of their family overnight.

Vonnegut published *The Sirens of Titan; Mother Night; Cat's Cradle; God Bless You, Mr. Rosewater;* and *Slaughterhouse-Five.* In these books, he mastered his trademark black comic voice, making his audience laugh despite the horrors he described. Although he had become one of the most famous writers on earth, the 1970s proved difficult for Vonnegut. After his children grew up and left home, his long marriage to Jane fell apart. He moved alone from Cape Cod to New York City. In the coming years, he wrote *Breakfast of Champions* and *Slapstick.* His 1979 marriage to photographer Jill Krementz formalized their relationship of several years. They adopted a child, Lily Vonnegut. He wrote *Jailbird, Deadeye Dick, Bluebeard, Galapagos, Palm Sunday, Timequake,* and *A Man Without a Country.*

Throughout the 1980s and 1990s, Vonnegut acted as a powerful spokesman for the preservation of our constitutional freedoms, for nuclear arms control, and for the protection of the earth's fragile biosphere.

Kurt Vonnegut died on April 11, 2007 after a fall on the steps of his New York brownstone. He was mourned the world over as one of the great American writers of the second half of the twentieth century.

— RODNEY ALLEN

Letter from the Editor

There are reasons we continue to publish those who are not among us, meaning, walking around, meaning, sitting down at our sides, meaning, breathing, but who remain among us as long as their works are still alive. Meaning: meaning. There are reasons we continue printing the dead, alongside the living, who mean as much or as little. There are reasons we truly enjoy placing those whose meanings have not been shared so much, alongside those who are so well-known, whose readership is so large, that their meaning is dispersed as if almost all around us. We like to print the Big Names alongside the new. This is not some feel-good effort to give hope to the unknown creative types among us, by placing their works alongside those of a canonized icon. This is not done just to give someone out there a sense of accomplishment or encouragement. These are pleasant consequences, we are sure. But there is really more to it than this, we think.

We are meant to be creative. Either we are created in the image of a great Creator, a great Being, a great God, of this universe — yes, the One who gave us the rattlesnake, as Vonnegut points out: that One: the One we sometimes wonder about. Or that idea of a great Creator of the Universe is a product of our own imaginations. And every variation of it — every variation of that version of that story or truth most familiar to an Occidental steeped in the Judeo-Christian tradition or atmosphere — every other alternative to it, from India, from China, from Africa — every version of that creation story, if not true, is then a product of our own, human, creative, artful, beautiful and terrible, imaginations.

If the former choice in this either/or is true, if that creation story is true, then it follows that if we are created in the Image of this Creator, the least we can say, with certainty, is that, like the Creator who used his creation as the model, we too must be creative. We must be. One can argue about omniscience, omnipotence, or benevolence and all-goodness. But if the story is true, a creator created us in the creator's image, and the one thing and only thing we know from those sparse facts is that the creator created, and creates, and so, in the creator's image, we also are meant to create. It's the only part of "his" (or "her") image we can gather, from the premise.

If the latter is true — if those creation myths are just that — just myths … then those stories themselves, that notion itself, is a product of our *own* imagination. We have created the creation myths ourselves, in that case. In this case, taking this alternative from the above either/or, then every one of these myths, each of these concocted tales, constitute evidence: empirically verifiable evidence, rationally analyzable evidence. They prove, just the same, that we create. That we imagine. That we make shit up.

Any claim of the form *Either A or Not A* is always true. It's a *tautology*. It's irrefutable.

So: given the above, it follows that, either with or without a God, we are still what Mr. Vonnegut would call *dancing animals*. We are creators either way. Obviously it's the destructive shit that goes against our natures. We are at home on the dance floor. At home in the choir. At home on the stage. And lost on the battlefield.

The reason we publish the dead, alongside the living, the great and established, alongside the struggling, the beginning, the unknown, or the new, who daily give something of themselves, and who remain until now relatively un-discovered, is because it shows that the creative act goes on and on . . . it is always happening, even in the most destructive of times.

This is something we want to show. We believe it. We believe Vonnegut believed it. And this journal, with each issue, as well as the library that gave rise to it, are meant to reflect back upon, and to respect, the life and creative legacy of Kurt Vonnegut. And Vonnegut, as already noted, had some very relevant things to say about creation — not only this vast and great Work-in-progress we take part in daily — but also every individual act that mirrors the same.

We are dancing animals. We are meant to write a poem, even a bad one. We are meant to produce plays, write novels, and make music. Music: the only proof Vonnegut ever needed for the existence of God.

We are meant to *make* believe, if not believe.

So if our first issue reflected back on the Vonnegut who finally, over twenty years, wrote his way out of Dresden, and our second issue reflected back upon the Vonnegut who made us smile, at the least, or laugh at the most, this issue is meant to honor the Vonnegut who honored, and who encouraged, the creative process itself, in all its forms and guises.

So thank you, creative persons. That's what we say in some of our rejection and acceptance letters: thank you for being a creative person, and not a destructive person. Even if we have not used your creative work, the act of creating it has already made you better, and has made all of us better as well.

So please: Enjoy.

This issue is for the creators.

Theirs is a light that never goes out.

J.T. Whitehead

Table of Contents

Notes & Acknowledgments 3
Kurt Vonnegut / John Clark 4
About Kurt Vonnegut / Rodney Allen 5
Letter from the Editor 6

from Past All Traps / Don Wentworth 10

ONE

from Kurt Vonnegut 12
The Pride of the Yankees / Fielding Dawson 13
It is Summer / J. Louis Gachotte 14
(independence) / Jennifer Thomas 15
The Bee Is Dead / J. Louis Gachotte 16
Davy Crockett Isn't Buried in Indiana / Cyril Wood 17

TWO

from Kurt Vonnegut 22
I turn my lovers into works of Art / Earl Carrender 23
Statement No. 2 / Kitrell Andis 24
"Too Much Realism" : Art's Newest Oeuvre / Wayne Hogan 25
modern art today / Wayne Hogan 26
Another Page in the Dictionary of Art: Impressionism vs. Expressionism / Wayne Hogan 27
I Should Have Been a Painter / Brooke Horvath 28
In the Land of Art / Anselm Hollo 29

THREE

from Kurt Vonnegut 32
from Selected Letters / Federico Garcia Lorca 33
Pleasure / Lois Ellison 34
Once Upon a Place / Chris King 35
(anti) Homer / Yassen Vassilev 36
10/22/12 / Lois Ellison 37
from The Hours of the Afternoon: XII / Emile Verhaeren 38
from The Hours of the Afternoon: XVIII / Emile Verhaeren 39
from The Hours of the Afternoon: XXII / Emile Verhaeren 40

FOUR

from Kurt Vonnegut 42
Emerging from War / David Cory 43
The Coffin / Donald W. Baker 44
The Driveway / Brooke Horvath 46
The Poem Stands on its Head by the Window / Bonnie Maurer 48
Poetry Lets Voicemail Pick Up 3 A.M. / Lylanne Musselman 49
Scrub Work / Maureen Deaver Purcell 50

Unentitled / Robert West 52

FIVE

from Kurt Vonnegut 54
salvation / Richard Vargas 55
Psychotic Imagist / JL Kato 57
Charles Bukowski: Erected / Kris Price 58
Homage to Jonathan Williams / Robert West 60
Luminous spaghetti with no beginning, no middle, no end, no suspense,
    no moral, no causes, no effects / Cassie Jones 61
A Cell Phone Rings during Matthew Dickman's Reading / Bruce Dethlefsen 62
Poetic Justice / A.D. Winans 63

SIX

from Kurt Vonnegut 66
hip gallerinas / t. kilgore splake 67
a certain male artistry / Lois Ellison 68
Kintsugi / Randy Brown 69
Distilled Music / JL Kato 70
Post-Impression / Clint Margrave 71
Going On: Backstage at Night of a Thousand Stevies / Kiara Downey 72
Ernst Ludwig Kirshner: Five Tarts, 1914 / Gerald Locklin 73
Untitled / Wayne Hogan 74

SEVEN

from Kurt Vonnegut 76
Hand in Hand Through the Greenery
    with the grabstand clowns of arts and letters / Nelson Algren 77
academic angling / t. kilgore splake 86
Un Titled / A.D. Winans 87
There's That / Robert West 88
The Rivals / Julie Kane 89
Dave Eggers's Writing Life / Dave Eggers 90
Rejection Flip / James Alexander Thom 93
Sand / Mitch Berman 95
The Fight They Wanted / Mark Wisniewski 97
Found Poem / Gerald Locklin 99

Contributors 100
So It Goes Circle 109
About the Vonnegut Library 110
Remembering my father / Nanette Vonnegut 112
Self-Portrait / Kurt Vonnegut 113
from Kurt Vonnegut 114

DON WENTWORTH

from Past All Traps

Leaves will reattach themselves

to trees before being a poet

will ever be more

important than

being.

ONE

Good examples of harmless toots are some of the things children do. They get smashed for hours on some strictly limited aspect of the Great Big Everything, the Universe, such as water or snow or mud or colors or rocks (throwing little ones, looking under big ones) ... Only two people are involved: the child and the Universe. The child does a little something to the Universe, and the Great Big Everything does something funny or beautiful or sometimes disappointing or scary or even painful in return.

— KURT VONNEGUT

The Pride of the Yankees

I GOT A LINE SINGLE to center which scored Mantle and sent Maris to third yet Dickey was waving me to take second. I had come in from center a little too fast, the ball hit my glove wrong, it bounced off my wrist and over my shoulder and went into center yet I had come across from left and covered as I came at the ball seeing me go into second, I picked the ball up with my webbing but of all things dropped it, I picked it up again and furiously fired it to second, my throw was to the third base side of the bag, but I caught it and pivoting with a kind of leap not to get spiked I slapped the glove across as I came in hard, knowing I was safe I made the traditional umpire gesture of safe which irritated me as I knew I had made the tag. I was wild in the stands. Maris had scored and as I came to bat I looked down to Yogi for the signal.

"Boy," Mantle later teased me, "it's lucky you goofed in center, you never would have made second."

J. LOUIS GACHOTTE

It Is Summer

(independence)

For tonight's magic trick
I shall time travel
myself back
to 1988
and search out
a stretch of yard
under
tall maple trees
and bravely take
into my shaky hands
a sparkler ablaze
with danger and promise
and I'll worry about
catching fire
because that's what my mom
said before she handed me
the sparkler
"watch not to set yourself on fire"
and so I stand cautiously still
as the other kids
spin about me
painting
the sky above and around their heads
And I will decide
to stretch the limits of my flammability
by waving my arm
across my own bit of sky
as I write
in light and smoke
JENNIFER
JENNIFER
JENNIFER
Except it won't say
JENNIFER or even JENN.
It will just
say
~~~~~~~
and look
like a bunch of
shaky squiggles
to everyone.
except
to me.

J. LOUIS GACHOTTE

The Bee Is Dead

Davy Crockett Isn't Buried in Indiana

When you live across the street from the cemetery, you make up stories to tell your friends. Stories about ghosts and dead people and weird people that walk through the cemetery at night. People in dark cloaks with their hoods up walking with lanterns swinging, swinging back and forth, and yeah, I saw that from the screen door of my house. And there was once the teenage girl, the one buried under the stone dolphin, she knocked at the front door and asked for a glass of water but when my mom got back to give her the glass she was gone. My mom asked me where she went and I told her I didn't know, I was playing. Mom locked the door then until Dad got home.

All of that happened. That cemetery is *definitely* haunted.

You tell people what you have to when the attention is on you for the first time in a long time, when everyone's gathered around you at recess and not pointing at you. In a way that people aren't making fun of the Scooby Doo shirt you're wearing, even though you thought it was really cool in the catalog and thought it was even cooler that your mom bought it for you, with Scooby Doo's face on the pocket square.

Because in reality the only thing you remember about that house is moving out of it, and your mom telling you to pick one toy to bring with you to the new house, not understanding that all of the other toys would be boxed up and be at the new house when you got there and you were bringing that one toy to comfort you, so you picked the rocking horse. And your mom said, "No, you have to leave that one here," and just *losing* it because you refused to go through life without your rocking horse.

"Ghosts? Absolutely, they were everywhere in that cemetery. I saw like thirty in one night, just walking around.

"My grandpa is buried there. I've never seen his ghost. I don't think he wants to be a ghost."

Luke started telling a ghost story, one that his uncle told him about seeing really bright lights one night out in front of their house. But when his dad went to check, they were gone. Luke was too young to remember that.

"That's not even a real ghost story," I said. "Those were just headlights. This one time, *my* uncle was staying down in the cabin we have in the woods, and really early in the morning he saw a lantern walk by one of the windows, then stay in front of the window by the front door for a long time. He took his gun and looked but when he opened the door the light went out and there was nobody there.

"He said there were two boys who used to live in the town up on the ridge behind the cabin, back in the 1800s — the pioneer times — and they got lost one night when they were hunting raccoons."

"People hunt raccoons?" Lacy piped up and broke the story.

"Yeah they do," Tyler said. "My grandpa has dogs that hurt them."

"Why would you hunt raccoons? They're so cute." Lacey said.

"They used to a lot," I said. "Now let me finish. It gets scarier."

"These two brothers were hunting and they fell into a well, because wells used to just be holes in the ground lined with stone, and now people see lantern lights a lot because they're ghosts and walking around."

And mine isn't a ghost story either because my uncle was drunk when he was staying in the cabin, going through a divorce during deer camp, which is really only an excuse to drink heavier than usual.

"You've lived in a lot of haunted places," Rebecca said.

"I have, but I'm not really afraid of ghosts. But they were really scary. My dog's even seen a ghost, I think. He got loose one day and ran around the cemetery, and when my dad finally got him back over he looked super super scared like he'd seen a ghost. Dogs can see stuff that people can't see, and we can pretty much only see ghosts at night," I said.

And my dog always avoided my father. He had a nose for booze.

"Who's all buried there?" Michael asked. Michael was weird, and he was just hanging out to try to fit in.

"Lots of people. There's one section way in the back with the fence around it with graves from like the 1800s. Like pioneers and stuff are buried there."

"Have you seen any pioneer ghosts?" Rebecca asks. I think Rebecca kind of likes me, but she's afraid to tell other people.

"Yeah, one. He wears a coonskin cap like Davy Crockett. It might be Davy Crockett, I'm not sure."

"Davy Crockett isn't buried in Indiana," Kyle says.

"It doesn't matter where Davy Crockett's buried, Kyle! He's a ghost. Ghosts can go anywhere they want. Duh."

"Have you seen all the graves in the cemetery? Even the pioneer ones?" Lacey asks.

"I definitely have. I spend a lot of time there." I didn't, though. The only graves I ever saw were the ones that belonged to the four people buried between the road and my grandpa. My dad told me about the old graves, the ones back in the corner of the lot, and he never said anything about pioneers. And he may have been thinking of another cemetery. He talked a lot when he drank, made stuff up.

"That's weird," Luke said. "Why would you spend so much time in cemeteries? Because only ghosts like you?" They giggled. Even Rebecca giggled.

"Just because I'm exploring it, Luke."

"Nuh uh. It's because you're looking for friends and you have to be friends with dead people. Your grandpa doesn't even want to be a ghost so he doesn't have to be friends with you." They laughed again. Harder.

Tears started to well up in my eyes, but I fought them back. My grandpa died a year before. No one else's had yet. My aunt had to come on grandparents' day.

"No, ghosts are just cool. They had a hard time in life and want to have a little fun before they have to go to Heaven," I said.

"Yeah says the guy who only has ghost friends," Luke said, and he laughed and spun the basketball in the air. He started to walk away and everyone else followed him. Followed him to go play basketball and even Rebecca didn't turn around and look back. So I stood there and fought back tears and wiped the couple that escaped on the shirt sleeve of my denim Scooby Doo shirt.

When the recess teacher saw me crying by myself she asked what was wrong.

But the bell rang, and I never said anything.

TWO

The arts put man at the center of the universe,
whether he belongs there or not.

— KURT VONNEGUT

The most useful thing I could do before this meeting is to keel over. On the other hand, artists are keeling over by the thousands every day and nobody seems to pay the least attention.

— KURT VONNEGUT

I turn my lovers into works of Art

It's more than they deserve. Some of them are just conversations with four walls confessing all the things that went unsaid. Some of them are lies I tell myself for my own well-being. Some of them drown mercifully in a bottle of cheap wine. Some of them go up in smoke from the cigarette in my hand. Another bad habit I've acquired. Some of them just disappear.

Statement No. 2

"Art!   Art!   ART!":

A dog with a bark impediment

WAYNE HOGAN

modern art today

So much birthday-suitness.
So much … exposure.
So much outright hand-holding,
So much surrealism … really?
So much newness, blueness.
So much light. So much
    vanishing point.
So much … annunciation.
So much paper mache.
So much tactile thrill.
So much anthropologizing.
So much Mylar. (So little
    cadmium).
So much illustrated minimalism.
So much fragile twilight.

WAYNE HOGAN

BROOKE HORVATH

I Should Have Been a Painter

I am a poet,
I said, and I

was hoping you might
pose in the nude

so I might write
a poem about you—

just a few brief
& stark-naked lines?

But she declined. "No,"
she said. "And don't,"

she added, "even think
of using your imagination."

In the Land of Art

the artists
work on the art farm.

They store the art they make
in the art barn.

Once in a while, they take some out
and take it to the art store.

When the art store sells some,
they take their share
and put it in the art bank.

Then they take their art checkbooks
and go to the art inn
to have a good time.

Or take each other to an art movie
or an art dance.

They wash their clothes at the art laundromat
unless they are successful and rich and have
their own art washer and dryer
in their art basement.

When the artists take a trip
(an art trip)
they stay at the art hotel.

When they get sick, they go to the art hospital.
And when they die, they're buried
in the art cemetery.

And that's the life of the artists
in the land of art.

THREE

I keep losing and regaining my equilibrium, which is the basic plot of all popular fiction. And I myself am a work of fiction.

— KURT VONNEGUT

From *FEDERICO GARCIA LORCA: SELECTED LETTERS*

Summer, 1923

. . . . You have no idea how much I suffer when I see myself portrayed in these poems; I imagine that I'm an immense violet colored mosquito on the backwater of emotion. Stitch and stitch … like a shoemaker, stitch, stitching away, and nothing to show! These days I feel pregnant. I have seen an admirable book that someone must do and I would like it to be me. It is "The Meditations and Allegories of Water." … The water poem in my book has opened up inside my soul. I see a great poem of the water, somewhere between the Oriental and Christian, European; a poem where one could sing in ample verses or in prose, *molto rubato,* the impassioned life and martyrdoms of water … The river and the water courses have penetrated me. Now one must say: the Guadalquivir of the Miño are born in Fuente Miña and flow into Federico García Lorca, modest dreamer and son of the water. I should like God to grant me strength and joy enough. Oh, yes, joy (!) to write the book I visualize, this book of devotion for those who travel through the desert.

— *translated by David Gershator*

LOIS ELLISON

Pleasure

Now I see
I come to embody
devotion, to grow close
to the rigorous
fold of its vision.

And although I've learned
to practice rigor until
it is a form of pleasure,
I've never trusted
pleasure to hold
close to the fold.

You know how
life streams in:
nervous, exhilarating,
questioned,
uninvited; now I
have to learn to be
that inviting: a silver hook
that attracts the fit,
a sharp flash that
pierces composure.
Just now
the devotion released
In the catch.

Once Upon a Place

This big city once a place
of wild onions, a rabbit's pelvic girdle,
American feverfew,
false sunflowers. Starlings eat trash and bully
littler birds. I kissed a frog,
Prince Charming, I liked him better as a frog.
I saw that in the New Age

Yellow Pages. I made a coonskin cap for
my thirteenth stepson's birthday.
The best friend I made on the carnival is
from Para, Arkansas, I
made friends with her husband, we trade ideas
for poems, like: Do you like
sunny days with no rain, or sunny days with
a little rain? Talk things out,
what is left of wilder orders, Death Valley
pines, rummy blooms: I showed up
when they told me to, and I paid attention.

(anti) Homer

I don't want to live forever
in this impossible city
where directions are perverted
years furiously turn
and everything is incurable
where stairs are inverted
pyramids built upside down
steps lead nowhere
and streets turn in a circle
where yards have no entrances
corridors end in walls
and there are balconies
on which no one ever stood
where doors are made of stone
and windows closed forever
with their nothingness
opening inwards
I don't want to listen to the voices of the immured
I don't want to be immured
in this impossible maze
of false rebirth

10/22/12

the heat of one's life:
of course it distorts, but also
is at times
a paradise;
it arrives overflowing -
the world has no sides:
it's conductive, a chemistry
that causes one to bend
with a heedless abundance
prized
either way

EMILE VERHAEREN

from The Hours of the Afternoon:

XII

THIS is the holy hour when the lamp is lit:
everything is calm and comforting this
evening; and the silence is such that you
could hear the falling of feathers.

This is the holy hour when gently the
beloved comes, like the breeze or smoke,
most gently, most slowly. At first, she says
nothing — and I listen; and I catch a glimpse
of her soul, that I hear wholly, shining and
bursting forth; and I kiss her on the eyes.

This is the holy hour when the lamp is lit,
when the acknowledgment of mutual love
the whole day long is brought forth from
the depths of our deep but transparent
heart.

And we each tell the other of the simplest
things: the fruit gathered in the garden,
the flower that has opened between the
green mosses; and the thought that has
sprung from some sudden emotion at the
memory of a faded word of affection
found at the bottom of an old drawer on a
letter of yesteryear.

EMILE VERHAEREN

from The Hours of the Afternoon:

XVIII

On days of fresh and tranquil health, when
life is as fine as a conquest, the pleasant task
sits down by my side like an honoured friend.

He comes from gentle, radiant countries,
with words brighter than the dews, in which
to set, illuminating them, our feelings and our
thoughts.

He seizes our being in a mad whirlwind;
he lifts up the mind on giant pilasters; he
pours into it the fire that makes the stars live;
he brings the gift of being God suddenly.

And fevered transports and deep terrors —
all serves his tragic will to make young again
the blood of beauty in the veins of the world.

I am at his mercy like a glowing prey.

Therefore, when I return, though wearied
and heavy, to the repose of your love, with the
fires of my vast and supreme idea, it seems to
me — oh! but for a moment — that I am bringing
to you in my panting heart the heart-beat
of the universe itself.

EMILE VERHAEREN

from The Hours of the Afternoon:

XXII

It was June in the garden, our hour and our
day, and our eyes looked upon all things
with so great a love that the roses seemed to
us to open gently, and to see and love us.

The sky was purer than it had ever been:
the insects and birds floated in the gold and
gladness of an air as frail as silk, and our
kisses were so exquisite that they gave an
added beauty to the sunshine and the birds.

It was as though our happiness had suddenly
become azure, and required the whole sky
wherein to shine; through gentle openings,
all life entered our being, to expand it.

And we were nothing but invocatory cries,
and wild raptures, and vows and entreaties,
and the need, suddenly, to recreate the gods,
in order to believe.

FOUR

"The big show is inside my head," I said …

— KURT VONNEGUT

DAVID CORY

Emerging From War

DONALD W. BAKER

The Coffin

"all a poet can do today is warn"
— *Wilfred Owen*

There's no use writing this poem.
It will be bad.
It will stay unpublished and unknown,
except that, as usual, I shall read it
to my wife and a few friends.
I think of them on their feet,
clapping and whistling,
swearing never to join the Marines again.
For this is a poem written by me against war,
and that is how wife and friends ought to react,
accepting the artifact for the achievement,
ego for truth.
Actually, little remains to be said against war.
It's foolish, trying to add
argument, anecdote, or emotion
to what better poets than I
have already written.
And those among you not Nazis at heart
have no need to be told.
But by way of parenthesis,
in this dissertation on bad poetry,
let me give it the ring of the lecture hall,
let me make a statement of theme:
Nothing is worse than a war.

Pause, for wife and friends to applaud . . .
Thank you.
Yes, that's what this poem insists,
that nothing is worse than a war,
though I have been repeatedly and excitedly warned,
by professors and other experts,
that polemic stultifies art:
metrical brilliance, architectonical genius —
irrelevant, once your poem engages itself.
Too bad.
These are ripe times
for poems that speak against war.

I should have enjoyed annoying them all
by composing a good one.
You've probably noted the virtuosity
posturing vainly in back of this discourse.
Lines 10, 11, and 12, for instance,
quintuple vowel alliteration, triple internal rhyme,
and the whole poem,
with small neglect of intelligence,
a *tour de force,*
practically purged of metaphor —
except in that word "purged"
and one or two others, "ripe," line 35 above.
Ah, me!
The craft so long to lerne,
wasting itself on a poem so *engagé*.
Dear wife, dear friend, dear reader:
this poem, already too long,
raises, like war, a tough technical problem:
how, successful or not, to stop it.
A last line should click into place,
someone has said, like the lid of a coffin.
But there's no point in wasting technique
on a poem dead from the start.

So I'll let you end it, dear people.
Abandon your minds, for once, to imagination.
Imagine I've stopped.
Imagine I'm stepping aside
to let the professors rise and rebut.
Many things they will tell you, including this poem,
are worse than a war.
And who knows?
We're all rational, liberal, here.
They may be right.
But now, before hearing them,
why don't you test your technical skill?
Ready?
Begin.
Imagine the coffin.
Imagine the lid.
Imagine the click.

BROOKE HORVATH

The Driveway

Sometimes my wife assigns me poems.
You have perhaps read some of them
if you have ever read me before.

Today she asked for a driveway poem,
possibly in an effort to call my attention
to the driveway's disrepair, its weedy
cracks, the holes that fill with rain.

Consequently, I am sitting with notebook
and a beer in a plastic chair in the drive
beneath the overhanging mulberry
and apple trees. Looking up, I can see
the blue jays' abandoned nest and a few
late mulberries hanging on. Otherwise,
the driveway's purple with them.

We talk sometimes of redoing the drive
with either brick or asphalt (cheaper)—
this stretch of concrete where balls
were kicked or dribbled, our feet
leaving its pocked surface for effortless
lay-ups, where the girls played four-square
and hopscotch, skated or rode bikes
down its slight decline through apple shadow.

It's here when small they threw the I Ching
with ball and jacks, sat chalking pictures
the rain washed away. It was here
the Mother-May-I game heard round the world
was played, and here one October
the good witch was saved from burning.

It was here someone was granted the serenity
to accept what could not be changed,
and here a Northwest Passage to the backyard
sought during the great blizzard of '78.
Upon this oil-stained surface we invented
fanfaronade, first danced the fandango,
debunked phallocentrism, witnessed
the birth of the blues, waved lonesome
farewells to those who would not return.

Notice our driveway's gentle curves,
its willingness to offer itself
as means, as end, as pubescent
proving ground, heresiarchic haven …
how naturally the snarled garden hose
finds a home here, how sturdily
the ladder rises from this firmness
toward the always disappointing gutters.

* * *

My wife will be back soon, pulling up
until she reaches my chair and empty
bottle, but I am finished anyway,
poetry having done what poetry
can sometimes do: fixing in the mind
what is fixed nowhere else.

The Poem Stands on its Head by the Window

Even so, the poem cannot reverse the order of things.
The fruit bowl on the table spills plums,
blue and speckled, still ready to split their skins.
Brains still blow up at markets and blood rains the beach.
Coins knock and jangle, clocks collide, and a buckeye,
polished as childhood, slides from the poem's pocket
into the rivered shag. Guns, bombs, missiles still fly in its head.
The poem's feet flex a silent beat. Can the poem move a line
of soldiers aimed to kill? Change a word to stop the genocide?
The poem sighs, heaves, utters the moans and sputters
of earth, the lost vowels groaning—hearts jettisoning
from daily life. The poem has seen the blue marble fully lit from space.
So, what gives, the poem asks, rearranging roots, hands
     and feet and blood and
breath to accommodate a world of violence and wonder? The poem
floats on a blue scribbled ground and ochre sky,
     reaches like Jacob's ladder.
When can the poem come down, walk among the pineapple groves,
tupelo trees, the coasts of Maine and Madagascar,
under the mottled green leaves safe again to marvel at you and me?

Poetry Lets Voicemail Pick Up 3 A.M.

Poetry, my love, I courted fiction behind your back.
She was rigid with plots, hauling characters around,
too inattentive to swoon at pretty words.
Your absence leaves me blank.

Your form is the most beautiful I've laid eyes upon!
I will coddle you with cadence
and tempt you with metaphor, the ecstasy of enjambment,
secure you with rhyme and repetition.

I'm not devising a way to take advantage of your imagery.
You used to lay yourself naked on my empty sheets!
We were so well versed together!
Please don't leave me to the prosaic life, a structured suitor to bitter ends.

Scrub Work

At first, it's just the general look that begins to nag at me. Seeing it from the front hallway or from the dining room, feeding the dog or doing the dishes, it nags. Even when I cook a holiday meal, the whole family gathered with friends in tow, I wonder if it somehow taints the food I have so lovingly prepared. It certainly doesn't make for polite dinnertime conversation.

It's time to strip the build up and old wax from my kitchen floor. I understand the tools — the kneepads, the endless amounts of solution, the right size brushes and rags. I understand the toll on the knees crouched and bent and stretched out, crawling across the hard surface. I can sort of feel when the solution is absorbed and pulling at the scum, when the small section of flooring is gooey enough to begin adding a little water, ready for scrubbing. I know how to use the brushes according to the length of the bristles.

It's easier to rinse starting with broad strokes from the mop, pushing one direction, then turning the mop over to a cleaner side and pulling, then rinsing and repeating. This process reveals deeper issues in the grout and tile textures so I switch to a small sponge, the one with a rough pad on one side. It's slower to scour the deep marks, a little more tedious, testing the aging arthritic thumbs. But it's strangely satisfying going after the same mess and I find it's easier to clean as the years go by. I love watching the floor come alive again, showing me that the prettiness is still there and that I still have the power to bring it back.

Some floors don't get this kind of care. Some harder surfaces only get a broom but they shatter everything that lands on them, sending shards everywhere, shards that are sometimes missed in sweeping, shards that get stepped on later and draw blood. Some floors are waxed and waxed and waxed, so that all that even the closest friends see is the glare of perfection, like the farmer who only cultivates the part of the field that grows along the road and keeps every one outside the fence.

    I give my floor a little more care because it documents the people who've walked or stomped across it, the dogs that drooled on it, the Sunday roasts and holiday turkeys that dripped on it, the plates that were dropped or thrown on it. It's my life story.

    At first I wasn't sure a woman my age could, or even should, tackle the work again. Then I realized a woman my age has also learned a thing or two about how to relieve the pains that linger. There are some dark corners of course where stains persist, and I don't move the refrigerator every time. I'm satisfied to polish over these occasionally with the "long lasting shine" knowing it ain't all that long lasting nor all that shiny. But I leave them, like the wrinkles on my face, with all the other little regrets in my life. I'm comfortable with that.

    The work settles me somehow.

    It just takes a little elbow grease and a good pen. The key is to not over-dilute.

Unentitled.

This poem just didn't deserve it.

FIVE

I believe that reading and writing are the most nourishing forms of meditation anyone has so far found. By reading the writings of the most interesting minds in history, we meditate with our own minds and theirs as well. This to me is a miracle.

— KURT VONNEGUT

salvation
for Ray Bradbury

i was in the third grade
spending the weekend
at my Nana's when i found
my uncle's old *Playboy* magazine
laying on his bed in plain sight
i picked it up and flipped
through the pages
i knew it was supposed
to be a big deal from the way
grown-ups talked about it
but i have to tell you
i wasn't impressed
although i now had a
pretty good idea why
ladies were so soft
in certain places

the cartoons were interesting
but they weren't funny to me
and just as i was going to
put it down i came across
an illustration of a T-Rex
and since i was all about
dinosaurs i started reading
the text which turned out
to be a story about men
paying money to travel
back in time so they could
hunt the biggest baddest
meat eater ever to roam
the planet and when T-Rex
showed up some guy
got scared and ran off
stepping where he
wasn't supposed to

a squashed bug totally
changing evolution

the story struck me like
lightning and my blood
began to boil between my ears
i started looking for anything
the author had written
finding his books at the
local library as his words
and stories eased the pain
of growing up with a father
who i thought loved the needle
in his arm more than me

the next year my old man
o.d.'d and i sought comfort
in the pages of books
looking for something to step on
a bug to squash and turn back
the clock so i could start over with
my not-so-happy ten-yr.-old life

so i started to write stories
diving deeper into the
sea of words and language
until i couldn't come up for air
and that led to my
first poems

now
forty-eight yrs later
i'm still at it

and Ray,
you magnificent
storytelling S.O.B.

it's just me
apologizing
for how long it's
taken to say
thanks.

Psychotic Imagist

Doctor Bill stands beside a white hen, plucked.
Blood drips off his tie, his cuffs, his hatchet.
He laughs and tells of the last time it clucked
before he snapped the neck with one ratchet
of the wrist. The chopped head falls to the earth
for yellow dogs to lick. Nimble fingers
draw a scalpel across the naked girth.
Liver, stomach, intestines—what stinkers!
A cologne for a mad poet/doctor
who must speak to one more patient waiting,
a hypochondriac (he mocks her!).
He scrawls out a prescription detailing
a red wheelbarrow with feathers on it,
unable to write a decent sonnet.

Charles Bukowski: Erected

His father chucked his Words.
His crater face burst Words.
His typewriter castrated Words.
His beatnik friends beat Words.

He barfed barfly Words.
He orchestrated ordinary Words.
He factored factotum Words.

He drank his way in and out of Words
Up chucking crass Words.
Fondling, Birthing, Word after Word.

He fucked his way through Words,
With ugly Words,
Pretty Words,
Fat Words.

His Ham on Rye ate Words.
His Pulp farted Words.
His Dog from Hell defecated holy Words.

Words scorned him.
Words dragged away his wives.
Words ran people over.

His Postman mailed saggy Words.
His Notes of a Dirty Old Man ejaculated Words.
His Bone Palace Ballet chafed Words.

Words gave him Hot Water Music.
Words gave him the Most Beautiful Woman in Town.
Words gave him Bluebird.

Words, Words, Words.

His body pontificates no more Words.

But his Words
Now give me Words.

And,
I give him these words,

You Bastard.

ROBERT WEST

Homage to Jonathan Williams
inventor of the "meta-four"

there's only one thing
better than dying and
that's living you should
give it a try
if it just doesn't
suit you don't worry
there's always the dying
to go back to

CASSIE JONES

Luminous spaghetti with no beginning, no middle, no end, no suspense, no moral, no causes, no effects

BRUCE DETHLEFSEN

***A Cell Phone Rings during
Matthew Dickman's Reading***

please answer that
no I'm serious
it may be the call
you've always waited for
the one that will
change your life forever
the one that will
make all this seem
absolutely meaningless
please answer the call
we can wait

Poetic Justice

A poet publisher writes and asks me
if they have named a street
in San Francisco after me
or does one have to be dead
to have this honor bestowed on him

I write back and tell him
the city fathers don't name streets
after poets honoring them instead
with small alleys

I tell him
the only living poet
with a street named after him
is the poet Lawrence Ferlinghetti

ironic the spot chosen
is a dead-end alley
and a favorite spot
for north beach drunks to stop
and take a piss
after the bars have closed down
the moral is
don't envy those who have
an alley named after them
better to be pissed-off
than pissed-on

SIX

Which brings us to the arts, whose purpose, in common with astrology, is to use frauds in order to make human beings seem more wonderful than they really are. Dancers show us human beings who move much more gracefully than human beings really move. Films and books and plays show us people talking much more entertainingly than people really talk, make paltry human enterprises seem important. Singers and musicians show us human beings making sounds far more lovely than human beings really make. Architects give us temples in which something marvelous is obviously going on. Actually, practically nothing is going on inside. And on and on.

— KURT VONNEGUT

t. kilgore splake

hip gallerinas

bloody guitar fingers

playing another riff

lonely poet

staring in mirror

seeing pollack's ghost

watching colors dry

a certain male artistry

When Paul Gauguin carved intricate figures
into his headboard, did he think:
    one day I would love to die beneath them
and did that make the grip
of the carving tool
sweet?
Mortality is the trade of the exotic.
Lying in bed, legs misshapen with sores,
now he just watches as women leave flowers,
women
who take great pains
to bring different arrangements in everyday.
Far removed from his original offspring,
the immigrant sees this as a prescient dream:
the world quivers and blooms, but not
    from my advances.
His instincts know he's the helpless beast
his work has somehow neglected to honor
now that honor forces his grip.
Daylight presses back from his sheets
as he tries to guard the ties he's bartered.
Doubting or dreaming, he speaks
to himself of things which no longer
belong to a canvas
but have always belonged
to what guards the last flame.

Kintsugi

Ashikaga Yoshimasa sent the shards away with hope
that artisans could somehow fashion
a repair for his shattered bowl.

Lacquered gold now fills its cracks;
it is stronger in the broken places.

The helmet that saved the life of Army Specialist Tom Albers
was shipped off to the procurement program executive office.
After months of analysis, it was eventually returned

to sit in a trophy case.

Distilled Music

(inspired by Girl at the Piano: Recording Sound, by Theodore Roszak, 1935)

        sequence   of sounds

    slurbering in

        slow   synapses.

sensical revelations

hum   sim   shimmering,

then

    revolution.

        mercurial comminglings.

blitzkrieg through fingers.

hammers to strings.

trigger the ping, pling, lingle-ping,

a ripzip slivering

into an open mic.

squiggles in a groove.

O, etched ripostes!
                dance, needle, dance

Post-Impression

Van Gogh came to my class the other day.
I dug him up, dusted him off,
got him some fresh skin, some organs.

Almost as good as new, I got his
joints working again, his brain rewired,
Franken-Gogh we joked around

before I brought him onto campus.
Unable to grow any hair,
I painted an orange beard on him,

gave him a corn pipe, a straw hat.
I thought the students would be delighted
to learn what the world-famous Van Gogh

had to say about art and life
and the bittersweet throes of posthumous success—
but none of them knew who he was.

KIARA DOWNEY

Going On: Backstage at Night of a Thousand Stevies

GERALD LOCKLIN

Ernst Ludwig Kirshner: Five Tarts, 1914

He sure didn't glamorize
The profession of Streetwalker:
No "Pretty Woman" in this woodcut.

And if you think this was just
Satire of a more Sinful Era,

Cruise the Pacific Coast Highway
Through mid-town Long Beach
At smogset.

WAYNE HOGAN

SEVEN

I think it can be tremendously refreshing if a creator of literature has something on his mind other than the history of literature so far. Literature should not disappear up its own asshole, so to speak.

— KURT VONNEGUT

Hand in Hand Through the Greenery
with the grabstand clowns of arts and letters

"Dear Mr. Algen," a young woman writes from Wheaton (Ill.) College, " I am a freshman and am standing on the threshold of a literary career. What is my next move?"

"Your next move, honey," I had to caution her, "is to take two careful steps backward, turn and run like hell. That isn't a threshold. It's a precipice."

The girl appears to feel that she is about to be welcomed through the gates of that enchanted land named "The Smiling Side of American Life" by William Dean Howells; later to be packaged by Richard Nixon as "Our Free Civilization"; then telecast as Marlboro Country.

A smiling image yet sustained, in air-conditioned stillnesses, when summer is the season. Then Creative Writers' Workshops, poetry seminars and Festivals of the Arts will materialize midst campus greenery. The Failure of Hemingway The Failure of Faulkner The Failure of Whitman The Failure of Melville The Failure of Crane The Failure of Twain The Failure of London and The Failure of Wolfe will be revealed by one-book novelists embittered by the failure of David Susskind to invite them to a party where they might have met George Plimpton or even Allen Funt. Just *anybody*.

Perpetual panelists will clobber perpetually rejected novelists with symbolisms concealed in the work of other perpetual panelists. Manuscripts will be returned bearing the instruction: *Insert more symbols*. This can happen anywhere but chances are better in Vermont.

There a kind of Sing-Along-With-Mitch picnic-king who can sing for *For He's A Jolly Good Fellow,* impersonate Dylan Thomas and denounce Jacqueline Susann for commercialism while counting his own house, will welcome cash-customers to his lonely-hearts literary supermart in the hills of Vermont. DEPOSIT REQUIRED ON ALL CARTS.

The mock-up poet will himself assure Miss Wheaton that nothing stands between her unreadable novel and its publication except consultation with a publisher's representative; whose identity will remain undisclosed until she's coughed up tuition for a season of creative picnicking (including a pass to the company store). At so much *per diem*.

The company-store pass won't get her into Faculty Cottage because the Sing-Along Supervisor draws a sharp caste line between published and unpublished writers. Miss Wheaton won't make this elitist group because not only is she unpublished but she's not well-groomed enough to make up for it.

Well-groomed women, seeking sanctuary while a divorce-mill is grinding, will wheel up in Caddies. A Junior Editor, grown middle-aged in search of a self he'd loved and lost, will arrive by Mohawk Air bearing an initialed attaché case containing only a pinch-bottle of Haig & Haig and a signed copy of *Atlas Shrugged.* Poor girls from the Village will arrive in sandals, seeking a piece of the Establishment and higher heels. Pursued by studs, barefoot or finely shod; on the prowl for piece of anything.

The authoress of one nonbook will explain how she made it in a man's world. The editor of *Seminal,* a quarterly financed by his mother-in-law, will not reveal how he made it in a woman's world. Then virgins budding between hard-covers, and paperback editors mildewing between soft, poor girls afoot and old girls a-wheeling, Discover-Me-And-I'll-Discover-You Faculty Wonders, a subscriber to The Famous Writers School who claims he wants Max Shulman's autograph (that *must* be a put-on), one-bookers, non-bookers, publishers' representatives, pinch-bottle vets, Miss Wheaton Supermart Dante and all, will spring hand-in-hand through the greenery and up and down the hall.

For one week or two or ten.

But after the grabstand clown has checked his holdings and counted all the carts in Vermont, Miss Wheaton will be left standing within the very door where she'd come in — to marvel at the emptiness of her own cart.

At so much per diem *per diem.*

Where had that " Publisher's Representative" gone? Could that quickie in the greenery have been with nothing more than one more unpublished poet? If Breadloaf hadn't been exactly a precipice it sure as hell hadn't been a threshold.

"Good writing thrives like corn in Iowa City," Miss Wheaton, still perplexed, reads in the *N.Y. Times,* "where 125 of the nation's most promising writing students just signed up for another semester of agony and ecstasy at what is generally considered the best author's course in the United States — the Iowa University Writing Workshop."

A six-month deferment from the armed services or the chance to have a steady boyfriend free from parental supervision provides the ecstasy; the agony belongs to the parents footing the bills. For what is offered at Iowa is cover, concealment and sanctuary. Their parents' whole purpose having been to protect their young, out of their playpens and into their teens, from the winds of economic weather, the kids who come to the Iowa Workshop have never even been rained on, poor things. Their strongest passion is watching Batman and their greatest hope that they will never get wet.

"The mere fact that the younger American literary generation has come to the schools instead of running away from them," Prof. Wallace Stegner of Stanford assures us, "is an indication of a soberer and less coltish spirit."

Prof. Stegner says that exactly right. The younger literary generation has come on the run because it's cold out there. The sobriety, and lack of coltishness, constitute their qualifications for reporting fashions or sports; or teaching "Creative Writing" on another campus. They bespeak a readiness to be cowed in return for a stall in the Establishment barn; at whatever cost in originality. They will not buck. They will not roar. At times they may whimper a bit, softly and just to themselves; but even that they will do quietly. For what it lacks in creativity, the Iowa Creative Workshop makes up in quietivity.

"Are you one of the quiet ones who should be a writer?" The Famous Writers School asks the same question that the founder of the Iowa Workshop — himself a "Famous Writer" — is asking: "If you are reserved in a crowd you may be bottling up a talent that could change your life. If you've been keeping quiet about your talent, here's a wonderful chance to do something about it. The first step is to mail the coupon below for the free Writing Aptitude Test."

The second step is to unbottle your money and send us some.

The University of Iowa is a good place to go if you want to become a journalist, a linguist, a zoologist, a jurist or a purist. Its Creative Writers Workshop is a good place to go to become a tourist. For it provides sanctuary from those very pressures in which creativity is forged. If you want to create something of your own, stay away.

For if the proper study of mankind is man, it follows that to report man one must himself first become one. How is one to create something who has not, himself, been created? How is one to *make* something without first having been made into something himself?

The style is the man: the personality that is unformed cannot create form; the young man or woman who is unintegrated himself cannot integrate wood, stone or language. Nobody can become *anybody* until life has pressured him into becoming *somebody*.

And as becoming somebody is a solitary process, not a group-venture, so art is a solitary process — not a field-trip in pleasant company.

Why has the Iowa Writers Workshop, in its thirty-five years of existence, not produced a single novel, poem or short story worth rereading? Because its offer of painless creativity is based on a self-deception. The student provides the deception and the school provides the group.

"Writers in groups are with few exceptions the most impotent and pernicious of tribes to infest the planet," the playwright Ed Bullins assures a *N.Y. Times* interviewer, "it would be healthier for a writer to socialize with drug addicts than with a claque of hacks."

Had the *Times* man gone to the kids, instead of playing patsy to the brass, he would have learned what they taught me:

"It's a respectable way of dropping out." "The longer I hang on here the longer I stay out of Vietnam." "I had to find a school where I wouldn't get kicked out for bad grades — either that or go to work for my old man." "It may lead to teaching creative writing somewhere else." "Too many squares around my home turf. I was getting conspicuous." "There isn't anything I really *want* to do — but hanging on here makes it look to my folks like I do." "My parents keep pushing me to get married but I want to have fun and games first." "I heard they were going to reevaluate the impact of literary naturalism on American writing and I want to get in on the ground floor."

"Iowa City," the *Times* man reveals the workshop's advantages to poets who teach there, "is the place where a poet can relax in the knowledge that a regular paycheck will come in no matter how badly the book goes." That it can go badly enough to embarrass readers, without stopping a paycheck, is demonstrated by the founder-poet's own odes to fried rice.

Of the eighty-odd students whose work I read at Iowa at least thirty were too disturbed, emotionally, to write coherently, in any language. Only two used English lucidly; and neither of these was native-born.

This is not to put down summer extension courses in photo-journalism, science-fiction, writing whodunits, juveniles, or how to train your chihuahua to be an attack dog. Such workshops, can prove commercially worthwhile as well as being fun; and campus rates are usually more reasonable than those prevailing at Fire Island or Aspen.

Therefore pay no heed, Miss Wheaton, to Festivals of the Arts in spring, poetry seminars in summer nor " Creative Workshops" in the fall. Avoid hootenanies in Vermont unless you're paid to appear or own a piece of the maypole. What "poet" would be peddling rides on a wooden carousel in the hills if he could bring a horse-and-rider alive on paper?

Nor pay any heed to the professional critic. He is not a man who has succeeded in literature but one who has been defeated by it. He knows everything about literature except how to enjoy it.

The relationship of the writer to the critic is comparable to that of the jockey to the chartwriter. After the horse has been ridden, and the risk taken, the chartwriter will analyze, for tomorrow's bettors, a race that, for the rider, is forever done. What the rider has yet to learn cannot be gained from anyone who has not had the living animal under him.

If God can't help him, both jockey and writer know, neither chartwriter nor critic can. For it is the imminence of the actual experience, whether riding a thoroughbred or enduring the shock of reality directly, at firsthand, that make the findings of the critic or chartwriter remote to the rider or the writer.

Imminence of death or prison also makes sharper the outcast sharpie's eye. His freedom being dependent upon distinguishing between fox and hare, he becomes both hare and fox. Fear of the pursuer and compassion for the pursued become quickened in him; as they become dulled in those who are neither hunter nor prey.

"Why shouldn't a cheat speak well sometimes," one of Gorki's thieves wants to know, "when decent people speak like cheats?"

Between the year that James Haggerty assured us that the moral of the U-2 incident was "Don't get caught," and the year the Pentagon Papers were leaked, we became increasingly aware that people in government must sometimes choose between losing their positions or speaking like cheats. It should come as no particular shock, therefore, that those whose hands control levers in the American literary establishment may become most outspoken for respectability when their own operations become disreputable.

"What this novelist wants to say," one lever-puller becomes suspicious of a novel wherein respectability does not depend upon private proprietorship, "is that we live in a society whose bums are better men and women than preachers and politicians and otherwise respectables (*sic*). This startling proposition..."

What's really so startling about preachers and politicians lying as fast as a dog can trot? Or of "bums" being better men and women than these same "otherwise respectables"? The designation of itself, by the American middle-class, as "decent," and of the unpropertied as "bums," is demonstrated by this "critic's aptitude for concealing that class's corruption while proclaiming its morality.

Why was it that nobody laughed when Malcolm X spoke; while multitudes chuckled when Hubert Humphrey wept on TV? Could it have been because, in racing his public-relations image from coast to coast, crying "You belong to *us!*" while clutching Lester Maddox's sleeve and, a week later, weeping stage-business tears over Martin Luther King's casket, that all Humphrey achieved was a demonstration of how weak and joyless a politician can appear while preaching strength through joy? Wasn't his failure to reach people due, at least in part, to the recollection of Malcolm X achieving strength through anguish?

"The strength of any nation lies in the children of its street-corners, its poolrooms and prisons and its alleys," Malcolm X had already forewarned us, "not in the power of its technology."

The direction Mr. Bullins points to young writers, out of the establishment and onto the street-corners, is therefore sounder than Prof. Stegner's confidence in campus sanctuaries.

Prof. Stegner is laboring under the illusion, common to academics, that a knowledge of the best that has been thought and said has a compassionating impact on the human spirit: a premise of American criticism since the days of the Transcendentalists; who came up with their best ideas under a campus moon.

That a dedication to the printed word may conceal an indifference toward cruelty; and that understanding of justice and human dignity becomes enfeebled in proportion to one's sophistication should be obvious by now. Unless we've forgotten that it was scholars well-disciplined in Shakespeare, Hegel, Goethe, Freud, Marx, Dante and Darwin, who yet devised the cultural programs at Auschwitz.

For the most dangerous societies are not those whose tribesmen sacrifice a bear to appease their gods; nor whose gurus distinguish themselves by caking their skins with ocher-colored mud. More ominous are those foregatherings of begoggled PhD's, their skins caked by sun-dried erudition, most of them earless, who perform linguistics so magical that that which is unreal is made to seem real; that which is empty to appear full: that which is false to seem true. Sacrifices endured at such ancestral rituals prove bloodier, ultimately, than that of one stupid bear.

The secret of linguistic magic lies in forcing matter to fit the form; rather than permitting form to be shaped by the matter. Dr. S.I. Hayakawa's miraculous vision of the Chicago Police riot of 1968, as an unprovoked assault upon the just and well-restrained forces of law and order, is a classic example of a man editing reality to fit a personal ambition.

Dr. Jaques Barzun, pleading for retention of the death penalty upon the premise that Joan of Arc, given a choice of life imprisonment or of death by fire, would have chosen the fire, is thereby enabled to demonstrate that fire would have been *his* choice also. Which goes to show you how dependent intellectual integrity is upon who is handling the matches.

That a sane respect among men, one for another, has been preserved at all in this country is not owing to the Bomb-Em-Back-to-the Stone Age, Send-in-the-Marines Eye-For-An-Eye Otherwise Respectables, but by people speaking behind bars: Gene Debs, Cesar Chavez, Martin Luther King, Malcolm X and Phil and Dan Berrigan.

Jailbirds all.

That it has been Earth's dispossessed who have given Man his most abiding truths, from a conspiracy trial on the outskirts of Rome to the anguish of Solzhenitsyn, is an ancestral paradox now commonly accepted by writers, readers and critics alike. That outcasts may speak truth, however, still comes as disturbing news to the critic quoted above: one perpetually embattled in defense of mediocrity so long as it stays respectable.

A yearning for respectability, so tenacious as to be achieved only at the cost of sensibility, is revealed in a handbook for other churchmice working the Establishment while ostensibly preoccupied with the arts.*

"What then are the reasons for the connection between the study of literature and the contempt for success?" this critic inquires and answers himself: "The noblest of them is undoubtedly that the study of literature encourages a great respect for activity which is its own reward (whereas the ethos of success encourages activity for the sake of extrinsic reward) and a great respect for the thing-in-itself (as opposed to the ethos of success which encourages a nihilistically reproductive preoccupation with the 'cash value' of all things). To acquire even a small measure of independent judgment is to understand that 'successful' does not necessarily mean 'good' and that 'good' does not necessarily mean 'successful'. From there it is but a short step in the world to the ardent conclusion that the two can never go together, particularly in America and particularly in the arts."

Well, what would *you* do, given a choice of a nihilistically reproductive preoccupation of the ethos of success encouraging activity for the sake of extrinsic reward, or the thing-in-itself leading to an ardent conclusion? Wouldn't you rather watch Kukla, Fran and Ollie?

Laying out a dollar and a quarter for 262 pages done by a man who earns his living by the written word, then discovering that he has no stronger control of the English language than Richard Daley, is dismaying.

---

*_Making It,_ by Norman Podhoretz, Bantam Books, 1969.

What, in God's name, is the man trying to tell us by splintering prose into such uneven planks? Simply that writers must often pretend that the laws of supply and demand don't apply to themselves as rigidly as to businessmen. That's all.

While gentile kids were watching the Three Stooges, he reminds us, he himself was a Jewish boy who owned only one suit. Yet he made up his mind early that *he* was going to travel with the Fast Mensa Set, Jewish or *not!* And he rode the subway all by himself to Manhattan. And walked right into the goy registrar's office and told him right out he was Jewish and had only one suit. And that after he made it he was still going to go home over weekends! Then he got right in there and practiced talking to gentiles until *he* got to meet George Plimpton, too.

And he *still* goes home over weekends!

Yet, how dreary to explain one's life in terms of the distance between names on mailboxes. Never giving us a glimmer of the faces and forms of the home of his youth: how soundless, odorless and colorless a life it appears: like watching TV on a night when the reception makes ghosts of the players.

And all merely to achieve the editorship of a magazine with less impact than *Women's Wear Daily!* Isn't the life of any precinct captain who succeeds, after years of struggle, in becoming Ward Committeeman, more meaningful? At least *his* life has had an impact upon the living.

The philosopher who thinks only for other philosophers has got to be lying. When he loses concern for those unconcerned with philosophy he is no longer a philosopher: he is an occupant with tenure.

The poet understood only by other poets is practicing a kind of pharmaceutics without a pestle: merely devising a certain distinction for himself by filling prescriptions and calling them cantos.

The revolutionary who revolutionizes his life-style but not his life has no closer connection with revolution than Tennessee Ernie Ford, singing *I Believe,* has with heaven.

Those who believe true change can be effected by meeting force with force may as well be riding with Hell's Angels. Changes will come from those most reluctant to straddle a bike: those willing to sacrifice power they already possess. Changing from a Harley to a Honda won't get it.

The artist who paints with one eye on the approval of those with the leisure to judge, the hands to applaud and the funds to buy, and no eye at all for those who'd rather go bowling than own a Van Gogh, may well gain approval. Then the light from the street strikes his masterpiece and all his colors wash out. He'd forgotten that Van Gogh didn't seek approval.

The literary critic, devising his thought from other thinkers, yet never consulting those who never think, may feel strangely uneasy about some clamor, coming to him faintly from beyond his shutters. He senses that a coherent literature, emerging from that clamor, would diminish him.

Are you still hanging around the edge of that precipice, Miss Wheaton? Still not convinced that it's *not* a threshold? Still bemused about what your next move ought to be?

One move you might make, I'd suggest, is to avoid sleeping with people whose troubles are worse than your own.

Another is to avoid drinking when you're feeling sorry for yourself. If you do you'll be finding yourself in need of a double-shot every time you consider what the world is doing to a nice person like yourself. And, since the world begins working on you early in the day, you'll have to get stoned to the bricks just in order to get out of bed.

Then you'll realize there's no longer any point in brooding about what your next move is going to be. Because you will already have made it.

Given a choice, never do anything anyone tells you you *ought* to do: unless you yourself want to do it. Given a choice, *always* do what you yourself want to do: even though everyone else tells you you *ought* not, you *should* not, you *better* not — and God won't like it if you do.

Watch out for what people tell you God wants you to do. Given a choice between your God and your life, save your life.

If your God is a God that tells you *He* comes first, he isn't any God.

If He's the kind of God who tells you to save your life, you'll never get another; pay attention.

If you can, believe in Him. If you wish, pray to Him. But bear in mind that your God is not mine.

Save your life. God can wait.

t. kilgore splake

academic angling

buff colored volvo

faculty parking sticker

trout fishing outing

expensive graphite rod

fly box loaded

dry "ibids"

weighted "op cits"

Un Titled

a metaphor mated with

a simile after

an orgy with rhyme

on a cold starless night

and that's how

the Language School of poets

was born.

There's That

Be happy at least you're not one of those
whose every new book of slack verse or prose
comes wrapped in the most sycophantic applause.
A hot pile of shit feeds the flies that it draws.

JULIE KANE

The Rivals

There were only three contenders
For the great big poetry prize —
Two of the feminine gender,
My frenemy and I.
So we went to lunch, extenders
Of the peace pipe, civilized.

"You are so much more deserving,"
She said, "than little old me."
"I'm not fit to be your servant,"
I said, "at poetry."
Yet we both remained observant
For toxins slipped in our tea.

"If not this year, then later,"
My frenemy said then.
I said, "Once nominated,
It's only a matter of when."
But a lot can happen, waiting.
And how long — two years? Ten?

"But you know — I'm ten years older,"
She let slip over dessert.
"I've had melanoma!" I told her.
"My death is sure to come first!"
Then the room grew suddenly colder
And the versifiers, terse.

Dave Eggers's Writing Life

I've been avoiding writing about "The Writing Life" ever since I first heard those words about 10 years ago. When I hear them, I hear the voices of high school and college friends, of my uncles and my cousin Mark, who would have rolled their eyes and maybe punched me, gently, in the face, for even trying to weigh in on the subject.

They would say the phrase seems pretentious; it's pretentious to ponder the writing life, even more pretentious to write about it in a newspaper such as this one, with its history of doing the serious work of preserving our democracy.

By comparison, the writing life, at least as it concerns me, is not so interesting. I just re-watched "All the President's Men," which I do every year or so, and, every time, I marvel at how interesting Woodward and Bernstein's lives were at *The Post,* and how well the film explains the reporting process, its doggedness and randomness, and how great an excuse it is to get out in the world and ask every seemingly obvious question you can think of (What books did the man check out?), because you never know, you might bring down a government that has it coming.

When I watch that movie, I also think about how mundane my own "writing life" can be. For example, I'm putting together this essay, not in a bustling metropolitan newsroom, but in a shed in my backyard. I have a sheet draped over the shed's window because without it the morning sun would blast through and blind me. So I'm looking at a gray sheet, which is nailed to the wall in two places and sags in the middle like a big, gray smile. And the sheet is filthy. And the shed is filthy. If I left this place unoccupied for a week, it would become home to woodland animals. They probably would clean it up first.

And here is where I spend seven or eight hours at a stretch. Seven or eight hours each time I try to write. Most of that time is spent stalling, which means that for every seven or eight hours I spend pretending to write — sitting in the writing position, looking at a screen — I get, on average, one hour of actual work done. It's a terrible, unconscionable ratio.

This kind of life is at odds with the romantic notions I once had, and most people have, of the writing life. We imagine more movement, somehow. We imagine it on horseback. Camelback? We imagine convertibles, windswept cliffs, lighthouses. We don't imagine — or I didn't imagine — quite so much sitting. I know it makes me sound pretty naive, that I would expect to be writing while, say, skiing. But still. The utterly sedentary nature of this task gets to me every day. It's getting to me right now.

And so I have to get out of the shed sometimes.

One thing I do to get out is teach a class on Tuesday nights. Back in 2002, I co-founded a place in San Francisco called 826 Valencia, which does everything from after-school tutoring to field trips, publishing projects and advanced writing classes for kids from age 6 to 18. For the last eight years I've taught a class, made up of about 20 high school students from all over the Bay Area, and together we read stories, essays and journalism from contemporary periodicals — from the "Kenyon Review" to "Bidoun" to "Wired." From all this reading we choose our favorite stuff, and that becomes a yearly anthology called "The Best American Nonrequired Reading."

Sometimes we read things that are okay. Sometimes we read things that we find important in some way — that we learn from, but that don't particularly get us all riled up. And sometimes we read something that just astounds and grabs and makes its way into the bones of everyone in the class. A couple Tuesdays ago someone on the teaching committee picked up a journal called Gulf Coast, published out of the University of Houston, and he found a story called "Pleiades," by Anjali Sachdeva.

None of us had read this author before, so we read her story without any expectations. But one page into it, I thought, Man, this is a great writer. This is something different. This shows great command, wonderful pacing. The story — about septuplet sisters conceived via genetic manipulation — could have been told in a thousand terrible ways, but she's managing to make it sing. In the story, after the initial triumph of conception, the sisters begin to die, one by one, leaving Del, the narrator, alone and forced to choose between awaiting her fate or taking control of her destiny. The story seemed to me some kind of small masterpiece, and I hoped the class felt the same. But I knew to temper my hopes; often I love something and the kids think I'm nuts. This time, though, I didn't have to wait long to know I wasn't alone.

Gabby, who takes an hour-long subway ride from East Oakland every week to come to this class, was leaning forward, waiting to speak, practically holding her copy to her heart. Describing what she loved about it, she made an impassioned speech about connectivity, about the limits of science, about Del's search for a more human, even humble, path, and what this means to her, to us all.

Nick, who had brought his own little sister to class, was floored by the ending — how, in the final act, the protagonist reclaimed a life both made possible and doomed by science. At the end of the class, when we voted Yes, No or Maybe, all the hands said Yes and I went home feeling electric about the possibility of the written word. I don't need to be reminded of it all that often — I'd just read Philip Roth's "The Humbling," and holy hell, that guy, even at 76, can still write something so ferocious, kinky, horribly depressing and yet full of the manic mess of life! — but truthfully, any reminder helps. When you spend eight hours in a shed to get a few hundred words down, you need every bit of inspiration you can get. And the best place to find inspiration, for me at least, is to see the effect of great writing on the young. Their reactions can be hard to predict, and they're always brutally honest, but when they love something, their enthusiasm is completely without guile, utterly without cynicism.

And I thought, okay, the writing life — damn that phrase — it doesn't have to be romantic. It can be workmanlike, it can be a grind, and it can take years to make anything of any value. But if, at the end of it all, there's a Gabby who holds the words to her heart and rides the subway through the night, back to Oakland, thinking of what those words on a page did to her, then the work is worth doing.

Rejection Flip

One thing that will bring a smile to a writer's face is hearing another writer talk about his rejection slips. The smile is usually rueful or wistful; sometimes it's a smirk. When we talk about our rejection slips, we are family.

When I stand up before a classroom of strangers at a writers' workshop for a book discussion group, the best way to establish rapport is by telling them of my long experience with rejection slips. This is insider talk. It's confessional. They lean forward. They are delighted, perhaps encouraged, to hear that although I have more than a dozen books in print, I can still get rejection slips, and do. My personal relationship with those brutal little missives goes back half a century. But my first rejection slip was one of the best things that ever happened to me. Here's the story:

Before the age of 20 I had not intended to be a writer; I meant to be a forest ranger. But when I got home from Korea, I had some things inside me that I wanted to get out. So I wrote a short story (very short; about 900 words) about a baby the war left orphaned by a dusty roadside. I knew nothing about the magazine market, so I sent the manuscript to the magazine I had most recently read: The Saturday Review of Literature, a fine magazine but now defunct. Awhile later, I received a letter from the editor of Saturday Review. It was handsome, cream-colored, letterhead stationary, and it said:

Dear Mr. Thom:

Thank you for sending your short story, DUST. It is, I presume, a work of fiction, although it has a powerful and poignant feel of truth about it.

I regret to say that The Saturday Review doesn't publish fiction. If we did I would be proud to publish this beautiful, touching, tragic story. It is unforgettable. I wish you luck in placing it elsewhere.

Technically, that's a rejection slip. But it implied that I might be able to write well. If my very first submission evoked that kind of appraisal, perhaps I should keep at it. In effect, the first rejection letter gave me the stem, or esteem, to keep me going through the hundreds of less kindly rejections I was to receive in the years to follow.

Yes, I said hundreds. Eventually, I had rejection slips from just about every magazine I'd ever heard of, and could have papered my office walls with them. (I didn't. Too depressing a décor.) I got so many rejection slips that I began to think I was getting unsolicited rejection slips. It was as if all the editors in New York or Boston had been alerted that I might send something and were saying, "Whatever story you're planning to send, it is not suitable to our needs at this time."

I become a connoisseur of rejection slips. Some were classy, and reflected well on the publishers. Others were poorly typed out, on cheap paper. Some came with typographical errors or bad grammar.

Some of those I would send back, with a note saying they weren't up to my standard: "Thank you for sending me this rejection slip. Unfortunately, I must return it. It begins to lag in the second paragraph, and the conclusion seems somehow contrived..." Or, "After careful reading of your rejection of my story, I must recommend that you revise it, or seek the help of a professional editor. You seem to have trouble with punctuation and dangling participles. Sincerely....

"P.S. If you resubmit this rejection slip, please enclose a self-addressed stamped envelope."

Well, why not? I had as much right to dislike their rejection slips as they had to dislike my manuscripts. I worked a year on a book; it merited a thoughtful turndown. A professional rejection slip should be a little masterpiece.

A few other rejects among the hundreds were somewhat encouraging, and some led me on to revise and resubmit, some finally leading to publication of an article or short story. But in the 17 years before my novels began to be published, only one other rejection slip gave me as much satisfaction as the first one from Saturday Review. Here's how that happened:

> I have looked at your manuscript, which was in Mrs. _____'s office when I arrived. I regret to inform you that Gibson does not publish material of this kind.
>
> Sincerely yours ...

Imagine the satisfaction I enjoyed in replying:

> Your rejection slip is two years too late. Gibson already published the book. I do thank you for returning my old manuscript, though I must say it's in pretty shabby condition.
>
> Sincerely yours,
> J. THOM

Sand

My childhood friend R.Q. Morton, who recently hit it big with his fourth novel, told the audience at Books 'n' Coffee 'n' Stuff that his new story was called "Sand" and that — his eyes directly holding mine — it was inspired by someone he had known for many years. When Morton's on tour I take a couple of days off to go to all his author gigs here in New York. Sometimes I even take the Chinatown bus to catch him in Philly or D.C.

Morton's story is about a man named Morton lost in the desert with no food, no water, and to top it off? a broken ankle. Got maybe two days to live, but a week to the nearest human at the rate he's crawling. The grit forcing itself into all the crevices, the sun beating down on him, all of it described in glorious detail; Morton's come a long way since the days when we used to wait near the 7-Eleven, telling tall tales to convince adults to get us a six-pack of Colt 45. I bet I'm the only guy who still calls him Mort the Sport.

So the Morton in the story keeps crawling along, knees raw, sand scalding and enfolding and invasive — all very beautiful I'm sure. Behind the admiring smile I keep pasted on my face at Mort's readings I'm wondering, as always, When do I come in? I've skimmed everything he's written, looking for myself in his characters, pretty much in vain. But this time, Mort just told the world that this story was about me.

And Morton the character's meticulously detailed suffering continues with a sandstorm. He can't get away from it: sand under his fingernails, sand in his armpits, sand up his ass. He's at the end of his rope when a scruffy little wild dog with these mournful, understanding eyes shows up, guides him along, on through a desert night as cold as the desert day is hot, the stars hanging close like, I forget, chiclets in the sky? — hell, if I was any good at this I'd be the famous writer — the endless expanse of sand made bearable now by their companionship, human and dog, each half-dead, each sustaining the other.

My eyes kind of teared up. Through the years, I'd bounced around from job to job, watching from down on the runway while Mort took off. I guess being Mort's friend was my career, the only thing I'd stayed at and the only thing I'd done well. I'd been true, and now he'd painted me as this self-sacrificing loyal little creature who had saved him from the suffocating sand. Honestly, I was too emotional to listen how the story ended.

When it was over I rushed the book-signing line: "I just want to thank you so much for putting me into that story!" I hadn't planned what to say, but old friends, they understand. They get it. "And what a wonderful character, how fitting," I went on, the people in line behind me sighing impatiently. "So faithful, so, so… enduring."

"Ohhh…!" Mort said, his finger waving vaguely at my chest, as if working out an equation in the air between us. "You thought you were the dog?"

The Fight They Wanted

for weeks the ugly one had been phoning my apartment
after midnight & hanging up just after I'd

answer & now she opened
her desk drawer
pulled out a small
magazine flipped pages to a short story
pointed at a page she (or maybe the heavy one?) had
highlighted & said "here's proof you called a woman
a bitch"

"no I didn't" I said & she
said "yes you did! it's right there between your
quotation marks!"

here I could have talked about the differences
between authors & characters
or about irony
or about how any good
antagonist ticks most readers off

but it seemed to be a good
time to allow silence
so I tried that

all four of their eyes (the heavy one's were
smaller) forced me to aim mine
at the floor

"ARE YOU DENYING YOU WROTE
THAT STORY?" the heavy one asked

"BECAUSE IF SO
WE CAN GET YOU FOR
PLAGIARISM!"

what I couldn't deny was that she (& the ugly one) had
tenure & I didn't

"well?" the ugly one said "did you
write it?"

the floor
I noticed
was rather clean
mopped every night by a black guy who talked
horses with me when I'd stay late
to grade papers in my office & I now

wanted only
to appreciate his work but I glanced
up at the ugly one & said:
"Santa Claus wrote it"

"you're mocking my
authority" she said & she nodded toward
the heavy one & said "& I have
a WITNESS!"

the floor
was spotless & horses
might have been running right then at Belmont
the black guy enjoying them
even if the long
shot he'd bet appeared doomed

but I wouldn't see him
for 6 more

hours & it was now very
clear to me that there was something
horribly wrong about that

GERALD LOCKLIN

Found Poem

"Well," Larry says,

"I handed in my found poem."

"Yeah?" I say,

"Where did you find it?"

"*POETRY* of Chicago," he says.

Contributors

NELSON ALGREN (1909-1981) once said that "literature is made upon any occasion that a challenge is put to the legal apparatus by conscience in touch with humanity." He is one of the great and giant figures of twentieth-century American literature. He was the winner of the very first National Book Award for his novel *The Man With the Golden Arm*. He wrote numerous novels including *Somebody in Boots*, *Never Come Morning*, and *A Walk on the Wild Side*. His novels and stories often explored the urban poor, addicts, drinkers, gamblers, con artists, prostitutes, washed up and small-time boxers, and jockeys. According to anecdote or legend the tour he gave for Simone de Beauvoir of the "real" Chicago left her in tears. He was also very funny, which is another often overlooked aspect of his work. He was a private in the United States Army, and although he would come to ridicule and deride the Master of Fine Arts degree as a pursuit for creative writers on the premise that it was a short-cut for posers lacking the life experience needed to produce authentic work, he also taught with Kurt Vonnegut at the Iowa writer's workshop when the MFA program was still a relatively new and rare phenomenon. He would die within days of his induction into the American Institute and Academy of Arts and Letters.

KITRELL ANDIS served in the United States Navy from September 1969 through August 1971. He attended Butler University and Indiana University at Indianapolis on the GI Bill. The Summer Ho Chi Minh Died was serialized in pLopLop Nos. 4–7. Andis' novel *Bookstore* was published by GeekSpeak Unique Press. He has also published two collections of poetry: Hearts Make Fists and Like Paradise Only Different, both with GeekSpeak Unique Press. More can be had at KitrellAndis.com.

DONALD W. BAKER (1923-2002) was born in Boston and educated by the Worcester public schools, Brown University, and the Army Air Corps. During the Second World War he served as a navigator in the 382nd Bomb Group in the American, European, and Asian theaters. He taught for thirty-four years at Wabash College in Crawfordsville, Indiana, serving as Milligan Professor of English Literature and Poet in Residence, and died in Brewster, Massachusetts, in 2002 at the age of 79. He is the author of eight books, including *Fought By Boys: New and Selected Poems From War.*

MITCH BERMAN is the author of *Time Capsule,* which was named a *New York Times* New and Noteworthy Book and praised by writers such as Donald Barthelme, Ishmael Reed, Russell Banks and — yes — Kurt Vonnegut. Putnam nominated it for the PEN/Hemingway Award and the Pulitzer Prize. Seven of Berman's stories have been nominated for Pushcart Prizes; two received Special Mentions in the Pushcarts and another was named one of the 100 Distinguished Stories of the Year by Best *American Short Stories 2001.* They appear in six major anthologies, including *Sudden Fiction (Continued)* (Norton), *Voices of the Xiled* (Doubleday) and *Pow Wow* (Da Capo). Most were published by top literary magazines such as *TriQuarterly, Antioch Review, Michigan Quarterly Review, Chicago Review, Witness, Southwest Review, Boulevard, Conjunctions, Gettysburg Review* and *Agni*.

RANDY BROWN, in 2010, was preparing for deployment to Eastern Afghanistan as a member of the Iowa Army National Guard's 2nd Brigade Combat Team, 34th Infantry 'Red Bull' Division. After he dropped off the deployment list, he retired with 20 years of military service and a previous peacekeeping deployment. He then went to Afghanistan anyway, embedding with Iowa's Red Bull units as a civilian journalist in May-June 2011. Brown is a freelance writer living in central Iowa, where he blogs about military topics at www.redbullrising.com. His military-themed poetry and non-fiction have appeared in such literary venues as *The Pass In Review* and *O-Dark-Thirty,* as well as Volumes 1 and 2 of the *Proud to Be: Writing by American Warriors* anthology series from the Southeast Missouri State University Press.

EARL CARRENDER is a life-long resident of Indianapolis and a current graduate of the Butler University M.F.A. Program. He received his B.A. in English at Marian University. His work has appeared in the *Fioretti, BENT, Clever, Backhandstories,* and *Scissors and Spackle and Punchnels,* where he was a semi-finalist in the *Indiana Wants Your Story* Contest in 2013.

JOHN CLARK is an artist, writer, and co-founder of Big Car, a nonprofit arts collective based in Indianapolis. Big Car's mission is to bring art to people and people to art. Clark is dedicated to adventurous creative experimentation and collaboration.

DAVID CORY has been a Hoosier his whole life. He is a doctor specializing in diagnostic radiology, a skill he acquired at Indiana University Medical Center a few decades ago. In his day job, he deals with precise digital images of the human body made with very expensive machines. In his avocation of photography, he makes multiple exposures on film with an inexpensive plastic film camera called a Holga. This is his creative outlet. His contribution to this year's issue of *So It Goes* was made at Monument Circle in 2014.

FIELDING DAWSON (1930-2002) was, according to most accounts, a "beat era" short story author and novelist. He was more than that and was a master of the short story genre. His best short and long fiction work was reminiscent, simultaneously, of (1) a long-standing American tradition of an understated sense of humor and an understated love of humanity that goes as far back as O'Henry, (2) an emotional honesty and an emotional wisdom reminiscent of the best of Sherwood Anderson's better short fiction, and (3) a stylistic innovation that mirrors the Beats of his own time. Dawson was the author of more than 20 titles and was a "stream of consciousness" author before the label became officially recognized. Andre Codrescu has described Dawson as "wise ... deeply human ... and searching." Codrescu was right. Dawson was all of those. Dawson spent his writer's life from his home in Brooklyn teaching creative writing to inmates in the New York prison system, rather than fishing for accolades among the academics, in safety. Dawson was a cook in the U.S. Army in the 1950s, the worst of two, or more, worlds — if one thinks "cook" or "1950s" or "U.S. Army" — before attending Black Mountain College, an experience he captured eloquently and authentically in his memoir, *The Black Mountain Book.* Other well-known attendees and teachers at the now-famous creative arts institution, Black Mountain, included Charles Olson, Franz Kline, and Robert Creeley. Dawson is an under-recognized and under-appreciated gem in the history of Twentieth-Century American literature.

BRUCE DETHLEFSEN was born in Kansas City in 1948 & moved to Wisconsin in 1966. He was Wisconsin Poet Laureate for 2011-2012. His past works include *A Decent Road, Something Near the Dance Floor, and Breather.* Dethlefsen has been twice-nominated for the Pushcart Prize, and his poems have been featured on Garrison Keillor's "Writer's Almanac."

KIARA DOWNEY is a high school English teacher who frequently photographs and writes about performers in downtown Manhattan.

DAVE EGGERS is the author of six previous books, including "Zeitoun," a nonfiction account of a Syrian-American immigrant and his extraordinary experience during Hurricane Katrina and "What Is the What," a finalist for the 2006 National Book Critics Circle Award. That book, about Valentino Achak Deng, a survivor of the civil war in southern Sudan, gave birth to the Valentino Achak Deng Foundation, run by Mr. Deng and dedicated to building secondary schools in southern Sudan. Eggers is the founder and editor of *McSweeney's*, an independent publishing house based in San Francisco that produces a quarterly journal, a monthly magazine ("The Believer"), and "Wholphin," a quarterly DVD of short films and documentaries. In 2002, with Nínive Calegari he co-founded 826 Valencia, a nonprofit writing and tutoring center for youth in the Mission District of San Francisco. Local communities have since opened sister 826 centers in Chicago, Los Angeles, Brooklyn, Ann Arbor, Seattle, and Boston. In 2004, Eggers taught at the University of California-Berkeley Graduate School of Journalism, and there, with Dr. Lola Vollen, he co-founded Voice of Witness, a series of books using oral history to illuminate human rights crises around the world. A native of Chicago, Eggers graduated from the University of Illinois with a degree in journalism. He now lives in the San Francisco Bay Area with his wife and two children.

LOIS ELLISON was born in NYC in 1956. So many years ago, she received a BA from Oberlin College and an MFA from Columbia University. She lives in Brooklyn where she raised a daughter, and paints and writes.

J. LOUIS GACHOTTE is a 6th grader at Northview Middle School. If he is not in school or taking photographs, he enjoys playing baseball and hockey or farting around in an effort to avoid homework.

DAVID GERSHATOR has appeared in numerous anthologies and journals. He is a recipient of an NEH literature grant and New York State CAPS poetry award. He is Associate Editor, *Home Planet News*. His poetry collections include *Play Mas'* and *Elijah's Child*. For more information about his paintings, prints, and children's books, visit www.davidgershator.com.

WAYNE HOGAN once did an 18-month tour, U.S. Navy, in Guam. He is a self-taught writer and artist. His slightly off-kilter view of things is expressed through essays, short stories, and poems, and through the media of collage, acrylic, line drawings, and cartoons. His work has appeared in *The Christian Science Monitor, The New Yorker,* and *Country Living* magazines, and in numerous literary journals including *The North American Review, Bostonia, The Quarterly, Spinning Jenny, Abbey, Lilliput Review, Rhino, Nerve Cowboy,* and *Waterways,* and in books from Kings Estate Press and Swamp Press. Wayne was named "Writer of the Year" in 1992 by the Cookeville Creative Writers and "Outstanding Artist" in 2006 by the Cookeville Arts Council. Through his own little books press imprimatur, Wayne has published dozens of chapbooks containing his writing and artwork. These works and samplings of his visual art are available at Cookeville's premier gallery, ART a'la Carte.

ANSELM HOLLO (1934-2013), was a Finnish poet and translator, who lived in the United States from 1967 until his death in 2013. Hollo translated works from the Swedish, Finnish, German, and French into English. Hollo was the author of more than 40 published books of poetry in English. His father was a philosophy professor, and Hollo's work itself is often philosophical, but other noted influences include the Beats. He is, ultimately, however, too unique to classify and too unique for anyone to attribute his work to school, upbringing, style, or influence. In 2001, according to standard biography, Hollo was elected to the honorary position of "anti-poet laureate." Hollo also taught creative writing at a number of institutions, including SUNY Buffalo, the Iowa Writer's Workshop (where Kurt Vonnegut also once taught), and, from 1985 until his death, the Jack Kerouac School of Disembodied Poetics, at Nairopa University, where Hollo was a full professor.

BROOKE HORVATH teaches at Kent State University. He is the author, most recently, of *The Lecture on Dust* (poems) and *Understanding Nelson Algren*.

CASSIE JONES just received her MFA in Visual Art from Washington University in St. Louis. She is a native Californian with a penchant for plastic dinosaurs, the ocean, jelly beans and a good story.

JULIE KANE, born in Massachusetts, has lived in Louisiana for three decades and has written so well about it they once made her Louisiana's Poet Laureate, a position she has since relinquished. A student in Anne Sexton's graduate poetry seminar at Boston University, she has since gone on to win the Academy of American Poets Prize (Louise Gluck, judge) and the National Poetry Series Prize (selected by Maxine Kumin). She is also a Donald Justice Poetry Prize winner and a Fulbright scholar. Her many wonderful works, which employ the formal as well as the free with equal skill, include but are not limited to *The Bartender Poems, Body and Soul, Rhythm & Booze,* and *Jazz Funeral.* Look for her most recent collection, *Paper Bullets,* published by White Violet Press.

JL KATO is a native of Japan whose assimilation into American culture is so complete, he doesn't know how to use chopsticks. His book, *Shadows Set in Concrete,* explores the author's discovery of his lost heritage. It won the Indiana Center for the Book's 2011 Best Book of Indiana Award for poetry. His poems have appeared in many literary journals, including *Paterson Literary Review, Raintown Review, Arts & Letters,* and the *Tipton Poetry Journal.* He is a former newspaper copy editor. He lives in Beech Grove, Indiana, with his wife, Mary.

CHRIS KING is a writer, producer, composer, editor, translator, and moviemaker in St. Louis. He is co-founder and creative director of Poetry Scores, which translates poetry into other media. He is producing a boxed set of the music of Bascom Lamar Lunsford for Smithsonian/Folkways and overseeing the editing of his second movie, *Go South for Animal Index.* His most recent chapbook of poems is *The Shape of a Man* (Intagliata Imprints, 2012). His poems and translations have appeared in *TriQuarterly, Quadrant* (Balmain, Australia), *Black Renaissance/Renaissance Noire, Inc. magazine* (London), and on the *Enpipe Line.* He serves on the Advisory Board of the Center for the Humanities at Washington University.

GERALD LOCKLIN was a professor of creative writing, twentieth-century literature, and literary theory in the Department of English at California State University, Long Beach, from 1965 to 2007. He is now professor emeritus but continues to teach as a part-time lecturer. Once hailed by the late Charles Bukowski as "one of the greatest undiscovered talents of our time," Locklin is also the author of over 155 books, chapbooks, and broadsides of poetry, fiction, and criticism, and he has published more than 3,000 poems, stories, articles, reviews, and interviews. His writings are archived by the Special Collections of the CSULB library, and he is listed in the usual literary directories. Look for a new full-length selection of his poems (since 2008) from Presa Press and a new edition of *The Case of the Missing Blue Volkswagen* from Spout Press.

FEDERICO GARCIA LORCA (1898-1936) was a lawyer, playwright, poet and socialist. Lorca received international recognition because of his association with a group known as Generation of '27, which was an influential group of poets that arose in Spanish literary circles between 1923 and 1927, essentially out of a shared desire to experience and work with avant-garde forms of art and poetry. Lorca published his first work of prose by the age of 20, his first play at the age of 22, and his first book of poems at the age of 23. By any conservative estimate, by his young death at 38, he wrote no fewer than 35 works, including plays, prose works, and books of poetry. Lorca was shot and killed, or executed, or assassinated, depending on the language used by the authors of the history books, by the Nationalist (Fascist) forces during the Spanish Civil War, in 1936. His works survive in a number of translations. His poetry is available through New Directions, founded by the poet-publisher James Laughlin; excerpts from his letters appear here in this issue with their gracious permission.

CLINT MARGRAVE lives in Long Beach, California. His first full-length collection of poems, *The Early Death of Men,* is newly released from *New York Quarterly Books.* His work has also appeared or is forthcoming in *The New York Quarterly, Rattle, Ambit* (UK), *3AM* (UK), *Pearl, Serving House Journal, Word Riot,* and *Nerve Cowboy,* among others.

BONNIE MAURER received her MFA from Indiana University. She is the author of the following works: Reconfigured, published by Finishing Line Press, *Ms. Lily Jane Babbitt Before the Ten O'Clock Bus from Memphis ran Over Her,* published by Raintree Press and, for the second edition, Ink Press; *Old 37: The Mason Cows,* published by Barnwood Press; and *Bloodletting: A Ritual Poem for Women's Voices,* published by Ink Press. She was awarded a Creative Renewal Arts Fellowship by the Arts Council of Indianapolis in both 2000 and 2012. She currently works as a poet for Arts for Learning / Young Audiences of Indiana, and as a copy editor for the Indianapolis Business Journal. She is also an *Ai Chi* instructor.

LYLANNE MUSSELMAN is an award winning poet and artist. Her poems have appeared, or are forthcoming, in *New Verse News, Pank, Tipton Poetry Journal, Flying Island,* and *The Rusty Nail,* among others. She is the author of three chapbooks, and co-authored *Company of Women: New and Selected Poems* (Chatter House Press, 2013). Musselman lives in Toledo, Ohio, where she teaches creative writing and blogs for herself and for *Wheresthecat.com.*

KRIS PRICE has an A.A. in Behavioral and Social Sciences from Modesto Junior College. He is currently attending University of Montana, Missoula where he is studying Creative Writing and Film Studies. Kris was an assistant editor for *Quercus Review,* and *Snail Mail Review.* He is working on his first chap book. His work has appeared in *Penumbra, Emerge, The Fine Line, the Newer York Press, Diversion Press, PressboardPress, Crack the Spine, Eastern Point Press, Red Ochre Press, The Literary Yard, Ijagun Poetry Journal, The Oval and the Modesto Poetry Anthology, More than Soil, More than Sky.* He was awarded second place in Kay Ryan's Community College Poetry Project contest that she held during her term as the United States Poet Laureate. He has read at Lit Crawl in San Francisco for the Newer York Press, 2013.

MAUREEN DEAVER PURCELL is a writer and civic volunteer who lives in Indianapolis, Indiana, with her nearly-retired husband and ever-vigilant dog. Her three grown children live in the Midwest of the U.S. and the Midlands of the U.K. Originally a commercial copywriter in radio and later a feature writer for a company newsletter, Maureen now meets monthly deadlines for her church newsletter and semi-monthly with her Women Writers' group.

t. kilgore splake (born Thomas Hugh Smith, 12/8/1937) is an American poet, photographer, and editor. He has written and published 65 books of poetry and prose. Over 3,000 of his poems and photographs have been published in anthologies, literary magazines and art journals. He has been nominated for the Pushcart Prize at least 12 times. He has BA and MA degrees from Western Michigan University, and has been a high school teacher and college professor. He is the founding editor of the publication *CLIFFS Soundings,* an international blend of writing and art. He is a 2010 Purple Patch Award winner for his chapbook *facebook,* and as one of the Best Overseas Small Press Poets of the Year. His creative work is archived at the University of New York, Buffalo, Ohio State University, Northern Michigan University and Michigan Technological University. He lives in the Upper Peninsula of Michigan.

JAMES ALEXANDER THOM, a native of southern Indiana, served in the United States Marine Corps and is a veteran of the Korean War. He has been a reporter and columnist for *The Indianapolis Star* and a lecturer at the Indiana University School of Journalism. He contributed freelance articles for *Reader's Digest, National Geographic,* and other publications before becoming a full-time and award-winning historical novelist. Several of his Revolutionary War and Indian War novels are set in his home country in the Wabash and Ohio River valleys. His best-selling frontier novels, *Follow the River* and *Panther in the Sky,* became television movies produced by Hallmark and Ted Turner. He dedicated his Mexican War novel, *Saint Patrick's Battalion,* to Kurt Vonnegut, who encouraged him to write it. Thom is married to Dark Rain, of the Shawnee East-of-the-River Band, with whom he co-authored the novel *Warrior Woman.*

JENNIFER THOMAS was born into a modern nomadic family of radio disc jockeys. Jenny's childhood memories consist of moving vans, libraries, and movies. Over time, her vocalized quirks, whims, and thoughts became fodder for her father's morning radio show. Thus, for the sake of privacy and social self-preservation, she became a writer. Against all odds, Jenny has lived in Los Angeles long enough to acquire an adorable roommate and a slightly evil cat. She currently enters the world of fantasy and imagination on a daily basis

— as a preschool teacher. She has spent the better part of the past decade finding solace in Kurt Vonnegut's books, which remind her that she is not alone.

RICHARD VARGAS was born in Compton, California, attended schools in Compton, Lynwood, and Paramount. He earned his B.A. at Cal State University, Long Beach, where he studied under Gerald Locklin and Richard Lee. He edited / published five issues of *The Tequila Review,* 1978-1980. His first book, *McLife,* was featured on Garrison Keillor's Writer's Almanac, in February, 2006. A second book, American Jesus, was published by Tia Chucha Press, 2007. His third book, *Guernica,* revisited, was published April 2014, by Press 53. (A poem from the book was featured on Writer's Almanac to kick off National Poetry Month.) Vargas received his MFA from the University of New Mexico, 2010. He was recipient of the 2011 Taos Summer Writers' Conference's Hispanic Writer Award, and was on the faculty of the 2012 10th National Latino Writers Conference. Currently, he resides in Albuquerque, New Mexico, where he edits /publishes *The Más Tequila Review.*

YASSEN VASSILEV studied in the French Language High School in Sofia, Bulgaria, and in NATFA 'Krastyo Sarafov' where he obtained a Bachelors Degree in Playwriting and Screenwriting in June, 2013. His diploma work, *THE WALLED IN ONES,* was his professional stage debut at Nikolay Binev Theatre. It won its competition for new drama in 2011, was produced in 2012, and was nominated as a Play of the Year for the most prestigious National theatre award, Askeer, in 2013. During his studies he also released two poetry collections and produced and performed several spoken word performances based on the poems in the Theatre Laboratory SFUMATO. In 2010 Vassilev won the *Award of the Audience* at the *Sofia:Poetics Festival.* In the beginning of 2014 he moved to Shanghai, and he is currently a 6-month artist-in-residence at the SWATCH Art Peace Hotel. In the beginning of 2014 his most recent publication, *Poems by Bastian Bertello,* became the most-read text on the Bulgarian branch of Granta online magazine.

EMILE VERHAEREN (1855-1916) was a Belgian poet, art critic, and playwright. Verhaeren wrote in the French language, and was a founder of the Symbolism school, and was closely associated with the Neo-Impressionists. He was an attorney, and it was in law school that he met like-minded students, with whom he founded the revolutionary arts journal, *La Jeune Belgique.* Although Verhaeren was employed with a prominent criminal law practice, his frequent contacts with young radicals, artists and writers led him to abandon the legal profession and to dedicate his life to poetry and literature. As a spokesperson for the artistic revival in Europe at the turn of the century, he promoted or befriended (or both) a number of talents, including James Ensor, Paul Signac, and Theo van Rysselberghe. Verhaeren nearly missed winning the Nobel Prize for Literature (in 1911; won by Maurice Maeterlinck). Verhaeren was once described as "a unique personality, a whirlwind with an indomitable character, who did not bother himself with bourgeois rules, and who provoked or overwhelmed everybody with his straightforward directness."

NANETTE VONNEGUT has lived in Northampton, Massachusetts for more than 30 years. She was born in 1954, and grew up, the youngest of six, on Cape Cod. Ms. Vonnegut graduated from Rhode Island School of Design with a BFA in Printmaking in 1978. Somewhat reminiscent of her father Kurt's experience with SAAB automobiles, she once tried her hand at vacuum cleaner sales (Electrolux). In 1982, she married realist painter, Scott Prior, which turned out to be a good idea. They have three grown children, Max, Ezra and Nellie. Ms. Vonnegut's artwork can be seen at William Baczek Fine Arts. More recently she has been asked to write about her father, Kurt Vonnegut. We thank her for her permission to include a sample of such writing in the present issue, taken from her wonderful introduction to *Kurt Vonnegut Drawings,* published by The Monacelli Press (2014).

DON WENTWORTH is a poet who works in the single-breath form. His first full-length collection, *Past All Traps* (Six Gallery, 2011), was shortlisted for the Haiku Foundation's Touchstone Distinguished Book Awards (2011) and a *Small Press Review* 'November/December 2011 Pick.' His work has appeared in *Modern Haiku, Rolling Stone, Frogpond,* and *Bear Creek Haiku,* among others, as well as a handful of anthologies.

ROBERT WEST is the author of *Convalescent* (Finishing Line Press, 2011). His poems have appeared in venues including *Poetry, Christian Science Monitor, Southern Poetry Review, The Oyster Boy Review, Able Muse,* and Ted Kooser's syndicated column "American Life in Poetry." Originally from the mountains of western North Carolina, he currently teaches in the Department of English at Mississippi State University.

A.D. WINANS is the author of over fifty books of poetry, most recently *San Francisco Poem* (Little Red Tree Press, 2012). Winans returned to his native San Francisco after spending three years in the military, and he is a graduate of San Francisco State University. He was the editor and publisher of Second Coming Magazine/Press for seventeen years. His work has been published in over a thousand literary journals. A poem of his ("Lady Death") was set to music and performed at Alice Tully Hall in New York. In 2006, he was awarded a PEN National Josephine Miles Award for excellence in literature. In 2009, he was presented a PEN Oakland Lifetime Achievement Award. Winans has read his poetry with many noted poets including Lawrence Ferlinghetti, Bob Kaufman, and Jack Micheline. He is a member of PEN and has served on the Board of Directors of various art organizations, including the now defunct Committee of Small Magazine Editors and Publishers (COSMEP). He is currently an Advisory Board Member of the San Francisco International Poetry Library. His archives are housed at Brown University.

MARK WISNIEWSKI is the author of two novels, among other works. His second novel, *Show Up, Look Good,* was praised by Ben Fountain, Kelly Cherry, and Jonathan Lethem; his first, *Confessions of a Polish Used Car Salesman,* sold out two printings, after praise by the *Los Angeles Times*. His fiction has won a Pushcart Prize, and Salman Rushdie chose work of his to appear in *Best American Short Stories*. His poems have appeared in magazines such as *Poetry, West Branch, Prairie Schooner, Ecotone,* and *Poetry International*.

CYRIL WOOD graduated from DePauw University with a degree in English-Writing. He's the Creative Director at Metonymy Media, and resides in Indianapolis.

Kurt Vonnegut Memorial Libary
Board of Directors

Executive Committee
Thomas Holt
Matthew Knoy
Mark Lakshmanan
Kip Tew
Julia Whitehead

Board Members

William Rodney Allen
Fred Biesecker
Donald Farber
Daniel Griffith
Mark Lakshmanan
Marc Leeds

Kelli Norwalk
Joyce Sommers
Chris Stack
Mark Vonnegut, M.D.
Jane Wehrle
John F. (Jack) Wickes, Jr.

Honorary

Lewis Black
Linda Ellerbee
Andrew (Andy) Jacobs *(deceased)*
Michael Moore
Sidney Offit
Joe Petro III
Morley Safer
Kevin Schehr

Daniel Simon
James Alexander Thom
Edie Vonnegut
Martin Vonnegut
Nanny Vonnegut
Dan Wakefield
Howard Zinn *(deceased)*

Advisors

Bill Briscoe
Cathy Buckman
Terry Burns
John Cimasko
Corey Michael Dalton
Debra Des Vignes
Mary Jane Failey

David Hoppe
Len Mozzi
Rai Peterson
Daniel Sease
Diane Thompson
Kevin M. Toner
Magnus Toren

So It Goes Circle

The Kurt Vonnegut Memorial Library gives our thanks to the generous supporters of this publication:

LILLY ENDOWMENT INC.

AMAZON PUBLISHING

ANDREW POTTS

RAMJAC CORPORATION

ANN AND CHRIS STACK

JANE AND AL WEHRLE

JULIA AND J.T. WHITEHEAD

JOYCE SOMMERS

THE BALTIMORE CHAPTER OF THE
KURT VONNEGUT MEMORIAL LIBRARY

Would you like to sponsor next year's publication? Please contact Julia Whitehead at 317.652.1954 or e-mail julia.whitehead@vonnegutlibrary.org.

Kurt Vonnegut
MEMORIAL LIBRARY

About the Vonnegut Library

The Kurt Vonnegut Memorial Library is a public-benefit, nonprofit organization that is located in the Emelie Building in Indianapolis. In this small but charming facility is a collection of artifacts, books, and artwork that the late Kurt Vonnegut acquired or created throughout his colorful life. Not only do we offer access to Vonnegut's history, we also have a replica of Vonnegut's preferred writing space. Walls of books surround this area. A small shop offers t-shirts, Vonnegut's novels, and other stuff to the visiting public.

The Vonnegut Library strives to engage and inspire people of all ages to thoughtfully express themselves using language and visual arts. This is accomplished by connections with and support of art education programs and activities.

We are open from noon to 6:00 p.m. Monday through Friday (closed Wednesdays) and noon to 5 p.m. on Saturdays and Sundays. Admission and tours are free, but we do accept donations. Visit our website at www.vonnegutlibrary.org for more information.

Photo courtesy of Ball State University Photo Services

111

NANETTE VONNEGUT

"Remembering my father . . ."

Remembering my father and the house on Cape Cod where I grew up conjures up a cartoon tornado, a spinning funnel with dozens of floating Siamese cats, two dogs, a piano, a bucket of baby-blue paint, a grandfather clock, a garden hose, my mother wearing an apron, and my father holding a cigarette and a lit match.

My father was more than a writer: he was the guy who never wore socks with his off-white, banged-up sneakers, who rarely left the house and was very regular about disappearing into a forbidden part of the house called "the study." There were two doors you had to go through to get there. No one tried to pass through the second one. If you did, you'd turn to ash because the room was booby-trapped with something having to do with *creation*. My father had proven himself worthy to be in that room, although I always worried about what was happening to him in there. I could hear the rapid-fire rat-a-tat-tat-tat of his typewriter and knew he was trying to wrestle big thoughts onto small pieces of paper, rat-a-tat-tat-tat . . . tat . . . tat-tat-tat . . . At day's end, he emerged from his study and charged headlong toward the sound of my mother frantically cracking ice for his pre-dinner cocktail.

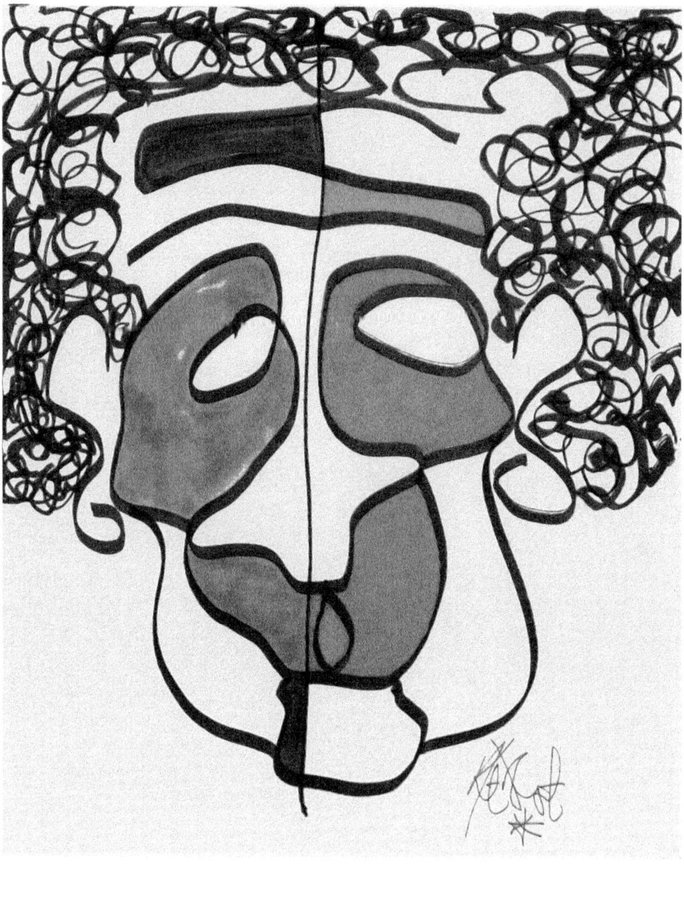

If you want to really hurt your parents, and you don't have the nerve to be gay, the least you can do is go into the arts. I'm not kidding. The arts are not a way to make a living. They are a very human way of making life more bearable. Practicing an art, no matter how well or badly, is a way to make your soul grow, for heaven's sake. Sing in the shower. Dance to the radio. Tell stories. Write a poem to a friend, even a lousy poem. Do it as well as you possible can. You will get an enormous reward. You will have created something.

— KURT VONNEGUT